MW00769628

BIRDS OF PREY OF THE WORLD

a Golden Guide® from St. Martin's Press

Written by Robin Chittenden

Illustrated by
John Davis/Wildlife Art, Ltd.

St. Martin's Press   New York

FOREWORD

This introductory guide to the fascinating world of birds of prey will help any enthusiast or student understand the diversity and beauty of these dinosaur descendants.

Golden Guides have a tradition of producing beautifully illustrated and well-informed nature guides, and *Birds of Prey* continues this tradition. Key species from every family have been selected, from the smallest Forest Falconet to the largest Eagle Owl. Interesting behavioral information, vital statistics, and ranges have also been included.

Special thanks must go to the artist, John Davis, for creating such excellent illustrations. He has managed to breathe life into these awe-inspiring birds.

I would also like to thank my partner, Olivia Lepri, for her patience and understanding while I took time out to write this book.

ISBN 0-312-32239-9   First Edition: March 2004

CONTENTS

WHAT IS A BIRD OF PREY?

Birds of prey, or raptors, are the only survivors from the time when huge meat-eating dinosaurs stalked the world. They are thought to be smaller relatives of these giants, evolving feathers and other characteristics that have enabled them to flourish right up to the present day. A raptor is a bird that has a preference for eating meat, whether dead or alive, although some species eat a lot of fruit. The term raptor comes from the Latin verb *rapio*, which means to seize, snatch, or tear away. Things that are raptorial are adapted for snatching or robbing. Birds of prey have been divided into groups (see Classification, page 19) and include hawks, kites, eagles, harriers, falcons, and vultures, which normally hunt during daylight hours, and owls, which usually hunt during the hours of darkness (nocturnal) or at dawn or dusk (crepuscular).

Raptors that have to kill and eat meat have evolved into efficient catching and dispatching machines. They have fantastic eyesight and some have a powerful sense of smell, used to locate prey. They all have hooked bills and curled talons for grabbing, killing, and cutting up their victims.

Many species of raptor are very territorial, ensuring that they have a large enough area of land to sustain them. Others, however, are more nomadic, hunting out high concentrations of food, such as swarming locusts.

Immature birds of prey are usually browner than their parents, which may reduce the chance of the adults accidentally attacking their young in the belief that they are potential contenders for their territory. The male is often smaller than the female, a phenomenon known as "reversed sexual size dimorphism." If there is a plumage difference, the male is usually more brightly colored.

Large raptors tend to get up rather late in the day in order to use the uplifting power of thermals so that it takes less energy to fly. Some can avoid flapping for hours.

Most birds of prey are monogamous, but there are a few exceptions, such as harriers, which may have several partners. Often, the same pair of raptors will return to the same breeding site and they may even migrate together. Certain species nest colonially, although some may only do this if there is a limited number of breeding sites or if their food sources are localized.

Raptors have cultural significance. In times gone by, they were important to the ancient Egyptian, Aztec, and Mayan cultures. Today, eagles and falcons are used by some businesses in their marketing strategy, reflecting the buying public's perception of the raptor's power and strength. Parts of some raptors are constituents in the ingredients of traditional medicines in Africa, the Caribbean, and China. Falcons have been trained to hunt for food by man for over 2,000 years, often resulting in the protection of the species to ensure a plentiful supply of birds for the falconers. In the "developed" world, raptors have been persecuted for various reasons for the past 300 years, a practice encouraged by bounties. In more recent times, habitat destruction, and pollutants have taken their toll. Despite this, only the Guadalupe Caracara has become extinct in recent times, although others are perilously close to dying out.

HEADS

Many raptors have a crest, while others have a white base to the crown feathers, which are raised when the bird is scared or concerned. Some have markings on the back of the head that resemble another pair of eyes, perhaps to confuse other predators. Falcons have bony baffles in their nostrils, which may help in reducing airflow through them during high-speed stoops. Some diving raptors have slit-shaped nostrils to reduce the entry of water. The ear openings are just behind and below the eyes and only visible on raptors with exposed head skin, such as vultures. Owls, and to a lesser extent harriers, have a flat face or facial disk that helps channel sound to their ear openings.

Because the Osprey hunts by plunging into water, its nostirls are slit-shaped and more horizontal than other raptors.

The Golden Eagle has larger nostrils as they don't need to keep out water.

EYES AND EYESIGHT

The eyes of diurnal raptors are set on either side of the head, facing forward. An upper and lower eyelid and a "nictitating" membrane protect the eye. Some species have a bony ridge above and to the front of the eye, which both protects and shades the eye. In owls, the eyes are situated at the front of the head and diverge outward slightly.

Lower eyelid

Upper eyelid

Nictitating membrane

The eyesight of birds of prey is between four and eight times better than that of humans. When scanning into the distance they can see eight to ten times farther than man. Some raptors can spot a grasshopper at 109 yards (100 m) and others can detect a vole or lizard at 437 yards (400 m) and a rabbit at 0.62 mile (1 km). Many owls hunt after nightfall, and although some use their exceptional hearing abilities to locate and catch prey, their eyesight in darkness is between 10 and 100 times better than man's.

BILL SHAPES

The bill is strong and hooked and is used for ripping up flesh into smaller, gulpable pieces. The sharp edges of the bill act like knives to slice through flesh. With the prey securely clamped under its feet, the raptor can pull off chunks of flesh by burying its hooked bill in the flesh and straining up and backward. Some falcons have a "tooth" in the upper mandible, used both to kill prey with a bite to the neck, and for taking apart insects. Some kites have two "teeth." The bird's beak, or bill, is made of bone and covered by horny plates of a tough fibrous material called keratin. Some have huge bills for chopping up large chunks of flesh, whereas others can have quite small ones for picking at little bits of meat. At the base of the upper bill is a soft, fleshy area known as the cere. The absence of feathers below the raptor's bill is for hygiene reasons, as they would get caked in blood and would be difficult to clean. Owls have beaks that are relatively small and are not generally used for pulling apart flesh as they tend to eat prey whole.

Peregrine

Egyptian Vulture

Snail Kite

LEGS AND FEET

Raptors' legs are used for walking, running, jumping, perching, and grasping, and often for killing prey. The legs and feet are covered with scales, and each foot has four toes. In most owls, the feet are not bare but are covered with feathers, as their feet do not become as messy as those of other raptors. Raptors usually have the first toe pointing backward and the other three pointing forward. At the end of each toe is a claw, or talon, which curves downward and is made of keratin. The hind toe and inside toe are especially strong, with longer talons, and are used to crush and kill prey. The other two toes are used for balance when perched or walking. The feet are adapted for the species' diet: those of raptors that hunt slippery fish can have spikes, while those of birds that prey on stinging insects can have extra-hard scales. Vultures have weak toes and talons as they do not need to kill and catch prey. Raptors such as the Golden Eagle, which carry large prey, have a particularly long hind claw. Some falcons use the hind claw to strike down other birds in midair.

Some raptors that catch birds in flight have the aid of an elongated middle toe, like the Sparrowhawk.

Eagle Owl foot: Non-fishing owls tend to have feathered feet.

FLIGHT SHAPES

If you spend any time bird watching you will have noticed that when you spot a bird of prey it is often flying. To help identify it when it is soaring up high, gliding away from you or dashing past, it is useful to observe its shape and size as well as the color of the plumage. Eagles, hawks and vultures, or buzzards, have long, broad, rounded or blunt-ended wings for soaring. Falcons have thin, pointed wings perfect for high-speed stooping. Some falcons have a broad base to their wings, which makes them excellent at soaring. Sparrowhawks and goshawks have short, rounded wings for making quick, agile flight maneuvers. Look at the tail shape. Is it long and thin, as in falcons, or forked, as in most kites? Although owls come in many sizes, most appear blunt-headed, with rounded wings and short tails.

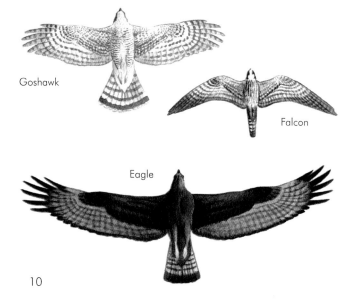

Goshawk

Falcon

Eagle

TAIL SHAPES

Tails are used to create lift and balance in flight, as a rudder for turning, and as a brake for landing. Tail shape and length vary in relation to how the bird catches its prey. Raptors that need to twist and turn through forest canopy tend to have longer and broader tails than birds that make mad dashes after their prey.

The kite's distinctive tail really helps this large bird to fly with great agility.

The buzzard's tail is a more typical bird of prey shape.

The kestrel's tail fans out to help when hovering.

STRAIGHT WINGS, ANGLED WINGS, AND CURVED WINGS

Raptors hold their wings in different ways depending on whether they are gliding, soaring, stooping, or flapping along. When kites and harriers flap along, their wings are swept backward and appear angled. Harriers also hold their wings up in a distinctive "V" shape when gliding, which is especially obvious when seen flying head-on. In contrast, kites, head-on, are similar in shape to a flattened "M." Falcons have long, straight, pointed wings in normal flight, but during stoops the wings are closed up against the body. Eagles and vultures hold their wings out straight when gliding or soaring, although, when seen head-on, slightly different angles can be distinguished. For example, when gliding, the wings of the White-Tailed Eagle slope down slightly while those of the Golden Eagle are slightly turned up at the ends. Owls have straight, rounded wings.

Harrier flight

Eagle flight

Owl flight

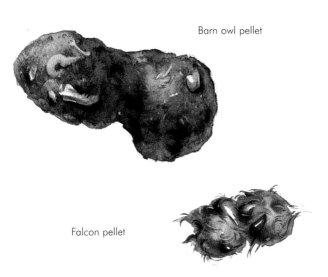

Barn owl pellet

Falcon pellet

PELLETS

All birds of prey and a few other birds, such as herons, kingfishers and curlews for example, regurgitate indigestible material. These are called pellets and are formed in the bird's gizzard. They can contain a mixture of bones, fur, feathers, bills and bits of insects. Fresh pellets can look shiny, this is from the coating of mucous the bird needs to aid regurgitation. Pellets are normally ejected within two days of the meal, although in some cases they can take up to five days. Some birds of prey are better than others at digesting small bones, therefore a pellet is not always needed. Scientists can learn a lot about the bird's diet from pellets. Sometimes you can find whole skulls, teeth, and many bones; this enables identification of exactly what creature the bird has eaten.

PREY

Prey is the meat eaten by raptors and can come from mammals, birds, reptiles, amphibians, and fish, or from nonvertebrates such as crabs, mollusks, and insects. The prey can range in size from a rotting elephant or blue whale carcass at one end of the scale, to worms and insects at the other. Most hunting attempts, except those for insects, end in failure, but after a successful attack the raptor will spread both wings over the prey as it feeds. This is called the mantling display and it may reduce the possibility of other species stealing the food. The fur, feathers, and other indigestible remains are regurgitated as pellets via the mouth. Research has shown that some birds of prey can reduce the numbers of its prey species within its territory. Some raptors are attracted by gunshots, in the hope of finding dead or injured prey.

Vultures feast on a dead cow.

ENEMIES

Birds of prey are at the top, or nearly at the top, of their respective food chains. Some smaller raptors have to keep an eye open for larger raptors with a diet that could include them on the menu. As with all animals, they can be prone to dying from diseases. The very recent collapse in the population of vultures in India is thought to be due to the spread of a lethal pathogen. The most significant threat by far, however, is from man, through habitat destruction, hunting, and the use of pesticides. Collision with power lines and moving vehicles can be added dangers. Surprisingly, despite these threats, no birds of prey have so far become extinct during our lifetime. Many, though, have come perilously close and still have a precariously low population. After massive falls in the numbers of some species in the second half of the twentieth century, many populations have recovered to former levels. Most birds of prey in the USA are protected by federal laws that prohibit hunting by humans. Conservation of natural habitats in which the raptors can hunt is vital.

The California Condor is possibly the most endangered bird of prey in the world. Once their greatest threat, man is now trying to save this species from extinction.

NESTS

The nest is used as a safe place to lay and incubate eggs and rear the young. Some birds of prey do not really build a nest but just lay their egg or eggs on a scrape on the ground or cliff ledge, or in a hollow in a tree. Others will construct huge nests from sticks and small branches, which are used year after year. New nesting material is added each year, so that after a few years the nests can become colossal and, in some cases, in danger of collapse. Some species will reuse abandoned nests built previously by other birds, including other raptors. Some nests are merely a platform constructed from sticks. Often a nest will be lined with softer material such as green leaves, small pieces of bark and moss, or covered with material so that they are camouflaged and therefore difficult to spot. Many species nest in trees, often in the crook of a large fork, while others will nest at the end of fine branches to avoid attack by predators. Many species of owl and some other raptors will nest in boxes provided by man.

Hen Harrier nest

Eagle nest

Owl box

HABITATS

Raptors can survive in any habitat, providing they can find enough food to eat and a safe place to roost and nest. As most habitats will pass these three tests, birds of prey are found on every continent except Antarctica, and can be seen in almost every type of habitat, ranging from Arctic tundra to tropical rainforest and sun-scorched deserts. Some species can even survive in urban habitats, and others will make use of man-made structures such as pylons and ledges on buildings for nesting. Some species of raptor can exploit a wide variety of habitats, while others are more specialized and restricted to one habitat. This is often a reflection of their diet. The least fussy eaters can survive in all sorts of habitat, whereas for others the choice is more restricted. The Snail Kite, for example, eats only a certain type of snail and is therefore limited to the freshwater marshes in which the snail is found.

MIGRATION

Many species of raptor migrate, including several species of owl. Migration is the movement from one area to another and enables the migrants to exploit new food sources as they become available, such as when the ice retreats in Arctic regions in summer. In general, species in the northern hemisphere follow the seasons, moving north in the summer and retreating back south in the winter. In some species one of the sexes can be migratory while the other stays put, and even within the same species, some populations can be migratory and others resident. They are partial migrants. Some species are nomadic, flying from area to area in search of food. When a good food source is located they stay for a while until the prey have been thinned out and then they move on.

Raptors often travel along migration routes, following ridges and coastlines. Large numbers can be seen in some locations, especially when they are funneled into bottlenecks, often where there is a narrow sea crossing. Many raptors do not like to travel over water. In general, small birds that can flap their wings for longer are less reluctant to cross open water. Larger species soar up high using updrafts, glide down, covering huge distances, and then use another thermal to gain height again. This method would not work over water, due to the absence of thermals, which develop only over heated-up land. Most raptors fly during daylight hours, coming in to land at night to roost.

Migrating birds are believed to have an "internal calendar" that tells them when to start migrating. Factors such as the change in the length of daylight each day will influence them. They navigate by making use of several bits of information gleaned from the earth's magnetism, the position of the stars, moon, and sun, and the low sound waves emitted from mountain ranges, as well as by using geographical features and, possibly, an inherited internal map.

CLASSIFICATION

Birds are vertebrates, or animals with a backbone. Other vertebrates are mammals, reptiles and amphibians, and fish. Birds can be separated from some or all of the other vertebrates by the following features: they have feathers, wings, beaks, and scales on their legs and feet; they are warm-blooded; and they lay eggs. They have been given a scientific class, Aves, which comes from the Latin word for bird, *avis*. Birds can then be further divided into different orders, two of which are birds of prey: Falconiformes (mostly day-flying raptors) and Strigiformes (owls). The Falconiformes are divided further into four groups, called families. These are the Cathartidae (New World vultures), the Accipitridae (hawks, eagles, harriers, kites, Old World vultures, and the osprey), the Sagittariidae (secretary bird) and the Falcones (falcons and caracaras). The Accipitres family has the greatest number of species. The Strigiformes are divided into just two families, the Tytonidae (barn owls) and the Strigidae (typical owls).

FAMILY AND SPECIES ACCOUNTS

For each species account, a vernacular (common) and scientific name is given. The common names are those in wide usage, although alternatives exist. The average length and wingspan is given in inches (in) and centimeters (cm).

CATHARTIDAE NEW WORLD VULTURES

There are seven species of vulture in this family, which live in North and/or South America. They are not related to Old World vultures but are thought to have descended from storks. They are all scavengers, living mainly on carrion, although some have a more varied diet. With their large wings for gliding and soaring, they can make use of thermals and updrafts to cover vast areas with minimal effort in their search for carcasses. They can go without food for long periods and have a large crop for bolting great quantities of food to tide them over any lean periods.

New World vultures do not build nests but simply lay one or two eggs in a safe spot. They will often form flocks and roost together overnight. They tend to have small heads in relation to their body size with no feathers on the head and neck, which would otherwise become caked in blood when feeding on carcasses. The naked skin on the head and neck is often brightly colored and used in courtship display to find a mate. Air sacs within the neck can be inflated to enhance the colors. This bare skin, together with their habit of urinating on their legs and feet, helps them to keep cool during the heat of the day. Sunning themselves in the morning allows their body temperature to rise quickly after the chill of the night.

TURKEY VULTURE *Cathartes aura*
length 27 in (69 cm) wingspan 67 in (170 cm)

A familiar sight in the USA and Central and South America, the Turkey Vulture is all black apart from an eye-catching red head and neck. The head and neck are black in young birds. Some birds migrate north in summer, although only to the northern USA. This vulture is very tolerant about where it lives, and can survive well in many varied habitats, from arid deserts to tropical forests. This may be partly explained by its very keen sense of smell and its ability to live alongside humans. It can detect decomposing animals even if obscured by vegetation. It searches for carcasses in flight by gliding on its long, pointed wings, held slightly raised in a shallow "V." It is such an expert at flying that it does not have to flap its wings very often. They can survive well without food or water for two weeks by living off fat reserves.

BLACK VULTURE *Coragyps atratus*
length 26 in (66 cm) wingspan 58 in (147 cm)

This is another all-black vulture, with white or gray feathers at the tip of the wing and black skin on the head and neck. Slightly smaller than the Turkey Vulture, it has relatively stumpy wings, which result in it being the least efficient of the New World vultures in gliding. It flies with rapid flaps followed by only short glides and is a common sight in the southern USA and in Central and South America. It does not have as good a sense of smell as the Turkey Vulture, often relying on them to discover carcasses and then following them in. It can spot its own carrion by flying at great height. With its especially large gape it can gulp down food more quickly than the other New World vultures. Its diet is more varied and it will eat live prey, including young turtles and even young pigs and calves, as well as bananas and avocados.

ANDEAN CONDOR
Vulture gryphus
length 44 in (112 cm) wingspan 115 in (292 cm)

A huge vulture with long, broad wings, this raptor breeds high up in the Andes in South America and is of great cultural significance to the local people. It appears dark from below, apart from a white neck collar, which is absent in young birds. From above, adults have a large, very showy panel of white in the wing, which may help individuals keep in visual contact over long distances. The condor scans the mountains for carcasses of mammals, including dead farm animals, and will also come down to sea level to scavenge for carrion among sea bird colonies. If the bird is threatened after a heavy meal, it will regurgitate some of the food to allow a quick getaway. Andean Condors have been killed in areas where farmers wrongly believed they preyed on their animals. However, they live over such a vast, inhospitable area that humans pose little threat; in some regions where there have been extinctions, reintroductions have taken place from captive breeding programs. There are thought to be many thousands surviving in the wild.

CALIFORNIA CONDOR

Gymnogypes californianus
length 46 in (117 cm)
wingspan 108 in (274 cm)

This massive vulture is on the verge of extinction and is restricted to two populations of released birds in California and Arizona. These were bred in captivity from the few remaining wild birds, which had all been caught near Los Angeles for the breeding program in the late 1980s. Others already in zoos were added to the flock. After successful captive breeding, the world population in 2002 was 198 birds. The released birds have matured and are now attempting to breed. It is hoped that successful breeding in the wild and a new proposed release site in New Mexico will bring this magnificent creature back from the brink of extinction.

The California Condor is a very slow breeder, laying only one egg every two years. The egg is usually laid directly on the ground in an inaccessible cave or ledge high up in the mountains. The egg takes up to 50 days to hatch and it is nearly another seven months before the young are ready to fly.

The adult is black with some white in the wings, and the naked skin on the neck and head is orangey-yellow. Its air sacs, the largest of any of the New World vultures, are used to display its lurid skin color. The immature bird has a dark neck and head. With the largest wingspan of any North American land bird, it soars over its extensive mountainous home range in search of its favorite food, carcasses such as deer and cattle. It eats up to 4.5 lbs (2 kg) of meat at a session, with the result that it will find it difficult to take off. It will wait until the meal is partially digested away or in an emergency it will regurgitate some of the food to allow a quick getaway. It is very reluctant to fly on wet or misty days and will simply sit at its roost site until the weather clears.

KING VULTURE *Sarcoramphus papa*

length 30 in (76 cm) wingspan 72 in (183 cm)

This large vulture lives in the forests and woods of South America and southern Central America. Adults are almost attractive-looking (for vultures) and have a creamy-white body with black-and-cream forewing and black tail. Most striking, though, is its orange-and-mauve head, with folded and dangling skin and piercing white eyes. Young birds appear dark all over. As it has a relatively poor sense of smell for detecting rotting flesh, it will follow other vultures to the carcass. It will eat almost anything, from dead cattle and sloths to marooned fish. It has a small gape and tends to nibble only slowly at skin and tough parts of the carcass.

Its heavy, powerful bill is perfect for opening the skin of larger mammals. Some of the smaller vultures have to wait for the Kings to do their work before they can feed. Usually only a couple of King Vultures and perhaps a juvenile will be seen at a carcass, possibly indicating that the species feeds in family groups and may actually have a territory from which other Kings are excluded. Sometimes many will gather around a really big carcass. The King Vulture population is declining as a direct result of forest clearance.

27

ACCIPITRIDAE FAMILY

There are 15 species in this family. They are usually large raptors with broad wings used to soar and glide in the search for carrion. With relatively weak flight muscles, they have to use thermals and updrafts to cover large areas. Many have naked necks so that blood from carcasses does not clog their feathers. They have distendable crops (except the Lammergeier) for gulping down large amounts of food. Some can live for up to 60 years. In India and Nepal, vultures are encouraged as an environmentally friendly way of disposing of human bodies. Sometimes special towers are constructed on which human corpses are placed for the vultures.

EGYPTIAN VULTURE

Neophron percnopterus
length 24 in (61 cm)
wingspan 63 in (160 cm)

This vulture is a summer visitor to southern Europe and the Middle East and is also found in Africa and India. It is a fairly small, dirty-white vulture with some black feathers in the wings. It has a yellow head and bill. Young birds are a dirty-brown color. It prefers open, dry countryside but often scavenges around urban areas and can travel up to 50 miles (80 km) from roost sites. Its bill is not strong enough to open up large carcasses so it eats small items of carrion, but will consume scraps from large carcasses, and will eat animal dung. It is famous for cracking open ostrich eggs by dropping stones from its bill to get at the contents, a rare example of an animal using a tool. It is usually solitary in nature, not often forming large groups like other vultures.

GRIFFON VULTURE *Gyps fulvus*

length 40 in (102 cm) wingspan 99 in (251 cm)

The Griffon Vulture's range is similar to that of the Egyptian Vulture. It hunts over large open areas and can survive in a wide range of habitats. A large, buff, creamy-colored bird, it has black wing feathers and a pale head and bill. Young birds are dark brown. It roosts in large flocks on cliffs, from which it makes use of updrafts and thermals to explore the surrounding area for carrion. Once one spots a carcass and starts to descend, the others will follow. It eats the muscles of medium-sized mammals, using its long neck to rummage about in the carcass. But instead of antelope and other wild mammals, much of its diet over much of its range has been replaced by dead domestic animals, such as goats. It nests in groups of up to 150 pairs in caves and clifftops. There has been some reduction in the species' population over some of its range due to poisoned bait.

LAPPET-FACED VULTURE *Aegypius tracheliotus*
length 41 in (104 cm) wingspan 106 in (269 cm)

This huge vulture, found in Africa and the Middle East, has dark brown feathers all over, apart from pale trousers and some white breast feathers. The head and neck are covered in bare, reddish skin, the color of which can vary depending on mood, temperature, and the age of the bird. It inhabits deserts with isolated flat-topped trees, on which it nests. It eats carrion from small to large carcasses and can consume up to 3.3 lbs (1.5 kg) at one meal. Gathering in some numbers around a carcass, it will boss about other species present. In fact it will often spend more time socializing with its mates at the carcass than eating, but will return later and use its heavy bill to eat skin and sinew. The Middle Eastern birds of Egypt, Israel, and Saudi Arabia are a different race. In Israel the Lappet-Faced Vulture is extremely rare and there is a captive breeding program in Tel Aviv to reintroduce the birds to the wild.

PALMNUT VULTURE *Gypohierax angolensis*
length 23 in (58 cm) wingspan 57 in (145 cm)

A red-faced bird with a striking white head and underside, and black-and-white wings and tail, the Palmnut Vulture lives in tropical forested areas of Africa, often by lakes, rivers, and seashores. It is unusual for a vulture in that, as well as consuming the occasional bits of carrion, it actually prefers to eat palm fruits, fish, crabs, shellfish, and tadpoles. It spends a lot of time each day in palm trees, pulling off the fruit with its bill and then eating it by placing it under its foot and pecking at it. It will often wade around in the shallows, searching for food. It nests in tall trees, building a platform lined with palm fronds in which it lays a single egg. Man does not persecute it as much as other vultures, due to its more vegetarian diet. It is often silent but will quack like a duck at roost.

LAMMERGEIER *Gypaetus barbatus*
length 43 in (109 cm) wingspan 101 in (257 cm)

This is a large, dark-winged bird with an oran-gey underside. The color is the result of iron oxide staining. It has a dark, wedge-shaped tail and is also known as the Bearded Vulture due to the black feathers that hang down from its face. It inhabits rocky, mountainous areas of southern Europe, the Middle East, central Asia, and parts of Africa. Eighty percent of its diet is made up of the bones and bone marrow of mammals such as rock hyrax and mountain goats. It will drop large pieces of bone, or even whole skeletons, from a height of 55–90 yards (50–80 m) onto flat rocks to smash them into bite-sized chunks, and will even drop live tor-toises and rock hyrax to kill them, often using a regular area of rocks, known as an ossuary. This behavior has given this raptor the nickname "bone-breaker." It has a more acidic stomach than other birds, to aid digestion of bones. It can also flap its large wings at injured animals to kill them or, more shockingly, to knock them over cliff edges, and has even tried this technique on humans. The Lammergeier

covers a colossal range in search of food and has never had a huge population. However, its numbers have declined in southern Europe, due mainly to poisoned bait put down in the last century to kill them. Captive breeding programs have been established to reintroduce the species, particularly in the Alps. In the wild it nests in small caves or protected ledges high up on vertical cliffs.

33

ACCIPITRIDAE HAWKS AND BUZZARDS
(True Hawks)
There are 58 species in the family known as "True Hawks." At their fastest when diving with their wings half closed, either for prey or in display flights, they can reach speeds of 62–125 miles per hour (100–200 km/h). Many have a transparent membrane that they can close over their eyes, and a bony shield across the brow, both of which protect them when they are hunting prey in thick vegetation.

BAT-HAWK *Macheiramphus alcinus*

length 18 in (46 cm) wingspan 42 in (107 cm)

The Bat-Hawk lives in Central Africa and Southeast Asia and, as its name suggests, it prefers to eat bats. It is an agile flier and will grab the prey usually from behind and above with its talons. The quarry is then transferred to the bill and is often gulped down whole, as this raptor has a large gape. Some lucky bats escape by biting the feet of the bird. It usually hunts at dusk and dawn, spending most of the day sitting bolt upright at roost in a tree. White eyelids and, in some plumages, pale markings to the rear of the neck may give the impression of an alert bird with its eyes open, thus putting off potential attacks by predators. It has particularly large eyes to help it see in poor light and they are outlined in white, making them appear even larger. The rest of the plumage is dark sooty-brown with varying amounts of whitish feathers on the breast.

● **CHANTING GOSHAWKS**
There are three species of Chanting Goshawk, all found in Africa. They are named for their chanting call of loud, melodious whistles, uttered during the breeding season.

DARK CHANTING GOSHAWK

Melierax metabates
length 18 in (46 cm) wingspan 37 in (94 cm)
This striking bird lives in moist, wooded savannah and open woodland in Africa and can often be found around rural villages. The adult has steely, dark, silvery-gray plumage above and is lighter below, with delicate dark barring. It has long, distinctive red legs and a red-and-black bill. The two other Chanting Goshawks are similar but have yellow-and-black bills and live in drier habitats. The immature bird is browner. This raptor perches upright on the lookout for reptiles, birds, rodents, insects, and carrion, then glides down and grabs the victim in flight. It sometimes follows ground hornbills and honey badgers for any potential prey they may disturb. It constructs a nest of twigs, which are sometimes glued together with mud and covered with spider's webs for camouflage. The nest is lined with mud and small bits of vegetation, which can include material from other small birds' nests.

● **GOSHAWKS**

NORTHERN GOSHAWK

Accipiter gentiles
length 21 in (53 cm)
wingspan 42 in (107 cm)

The Northern Goshawk is a chunky, large-billed bird with rounded and bulging wings. The female is the largest of all the accipiters and appears dark gray above and paler below with a black crown and mask through the eye, with a white line, or supercilium, above its eye, and white, fluffy feathers under the tail. It can occur in an all-white form. Immature birds appear browner. Found across the whole of the northern hemisphere, including North America, Europe, Siberia, and other parts of Asia, it lives in forested areas and favors spruce woods. Recently it has adapted to living in some parks in European cities like Amsterdam. A furtive species, it preys on medium-sized birds, including other raptors and owls. It has an impressive aerial display sequence incorporating stoops, rolls, and undulating flight. If intruders get too close to the nest, it has an aggressive display that can include hitting humans with its wings.

GRAY GOSHAWK *Accipiter novaehollandiae*
length 19 in (48 cm) wingspan 34 in (86 cm)

This largish accipiter is also known as the Variable Goshawk and, as the alternative name suggests, it comes in several forms, which all have short, broad wings and a large bill. It lives in the tall, wet forests of Australia. Tropical races are darker, having a blood-red front and blue-gray back, while other forms can range from being gray above and white below to being completely ghostly white. Its principal hunting tactic is to hide in dense foliage from where it spots its quarry, swooping out and grabbing the victim in its talons. It can eat a wide variety of animals, such as small birds, mammals, reptiles, amphibians, or even large insects. It constructs a flat nest lined with green leaves in a tall tree such as a eucalyptus. It is not particularly common over much of its range but has a greater population density in tropical areas. Although not globally threatened, the population in Tasmania has collapsed as a direct result of forest clearance.

39

● **SPARROWHAWKS**

EUROPEAN OR NORTHERN SPARROWHAWK

Accipiter nisus
length 13 in (33 cm) wingspan 26 in (66 cm)

This Sparrowhawk is found across Europe, Siberia, Asia, and parts of Africa and is one of the most common and widespread birds of prey in its range. It is a fairly small raptor. The male is blue-gray above and pale underneath, with rufous barring. The female looks like a smaller version of the Northern Goshawk. Young birds are browner.

Although most do not survive past their seventh birthday, the oldest recorded achieved the ripe old age of 15. It inhabits woodland and likes parks and cemeteries in towns. It eats small birds, which it catches with stealth and surprise, often using vegetation as cover, by dashing along hedgerows and woodland clearings, twisting and turning to outmaneuver the victim. This raptor will even follow its prey into cover on foot. It is usually solitary, but can be seen migrating in large, loose flocks in certain parts of its range. It constructs a stick platform near the top of a tree in which the female lays up to seven eggs. Its population has largely recovered following persecution in the mid-nineteenth century and another slump in numbers as a result of pesticide use in the latter half of the twentieth century. In Turkey and Tunisia it is trapped and trained to hunt quail.

AFRICAN LITTLE SPARROWHAWK

Accipiter minullus
length 9 in (23 cm) wingspan 18 in (46 cm)

The African Little Sparrowhawk is tiny, only slightly longer than a starling. It is the smallest accipiter. The male is very dark gray above and the undersides are paler with dark, reddish barring. It has two white spots on the tail, with a white band at the base. Females are browner. The brown juvenile bird has a white underside with large spots. A common species found in Southern and Eastern Africa, it lives in forests and woodland, often by rivers, and can survive in small patches of trees, including plantations in drier habitats. It hunts from perches, dashing out and maneuvering through the vegetation with great agility in pursuit of small birds, which are grabbed in midair. It will also tackle bats, lizards, and insects. Its nest is a stick platform lined with leaves and twigs and located high up in a fork of a tree.

SHARP-SHINNED HAWK *Accipiter stratus*
length 11 in (28 cm) wingspan 22 in (56 cm)

Found throughout North and Central America, this small hawk can survive in a variety of habitats, including wooded suburbia. Males are slate blue above and light blue below with a reddish-orange wash. Females are browner gray above. Youngsters are browner still, with bold breast streaks. One race of this species is migratory and huge flocks can swarm along migration highways, following ridges and coastlines. It prefers consuming other birds but will down small mammals, amphibians, lizards, and insects. The raptor catches its prey as it patrols its territory, or launches a surprise attack from its perch once it has spotted its victim. Prey is often plucked and prepared before being eaten or fed to young. The nest is rather bulky, and is built in trees surrounded by thick cover. Although not globally threatened, the population declined following the use of pesticides in the 1960s and '70s and as a direct result of woodland clearance. The two races found in Cuba and Puerto Rico are thought to be very rare.

SHIKRA *Accipiter badius*
length 12 in (30 cm) wingspan 23 in (58 cm)

This is one of the most common small hawks found in Africa, India, and Southeast Asia. It also summers in parts of the Middle East. The adult is blue-gray above with white and orangey bars below. It hunts for a wide variety of prey in woodland, savannah, and even suburban gardens, dashing out from perches within vegetation to grab its prey. Although its preferred morsels are lizards and small birds, it will eat insects, bats, and eggs. The female builds a small nest by herself, a task that takes about ten mornings' work. Constructed from sticks, which she breaks off from trees with her bill, the nest is lined with leaves and small pieces of bark and is located on a branch of a tree. She lays up to four eggs, which take about a month to hatch, and after a further month the young are ready for their first flight.

HARRIS HAWK *Parabuteo unicinctus*

length 21 in (53 cm) wingspan 46 in (117 cm)

This striking medium-sized hawk is exceptionally good at catching rodents. The adult is black all over apart from a rufous wing patch and trousers, and also has white tips to its tail with white feathers around the base. It is found in dry habitats in South and Central America and just reaches a few southern USA states. It has been reintroduced into southeast California. It will try and catch mammals up to the size of a rabbit and also eats birds, lizards, and insects. Hunting success is increased when groups of up to six birds cooperate by cutting off the escape routes of their victims. By grouping together, the hawks can also tackle larger prey than if hunting alone. The Harris Hawk builds a nest of sticks, lined with fresh vegetation, in a tree, a cactus, or even a man-made structure. The female often mates with more than one male, sometimes as many as five, a practice known as polyandry.

45

● **BUTEO HAWKS**

There are 28 species of *Buteo*, found worldwide except in Australia. Some species will hover to locate prey.

ROUGH-LEGGED HAWK OR BUZZARD
Buteo lagopus
length 22 in (56 cm) wingspan 56 in (142 cm)

This Arctic hawk breeds in the open tundra across the northern parts of North America, Europe, and Siberia. In winter it migrates south to avoid the Arctic freeze. The adult can show some variation in plumage but is dark brown above and paler on the head and underside, with a contrasting brown chest band. In flight it shows its distinctive white tail, with a black band near the tip, and its white underwings are outlined in black, each with an obvious black carpal patch. It hunts its favorite prey, lemmings and

voles, from perches or by hovering. The fact that lemmings form such an important part of this raptor's diet during the breeding season may be responsible for the three to four year boom-and-bust cycle in the population of these animals. The nest is a bulky stick structure perched out of harm's way on cliff ledges. The female can lay up to seven eggs in good vole and lemming years, although normal clutch size is between three and five eggs.

47

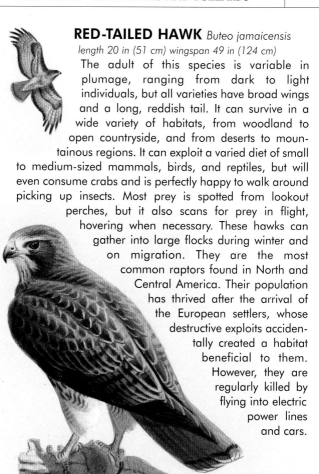

RED-TAILED HAWK *Buteo jamaicensis*
length 20 in (51 cm) wingspan 49 in (124 cm)
The adult of this species is variable in plumage, ranging from dark to light individuals, but all varieties have broad wings and a long, reddish tail. It can survive in a wide variety of habitats, from woodland to open countryside, and from deserts to mountainous regions. It can exploit a varied diet of small to medium-sized mammals, birds, and reptiles, but will even consume crabs and is perfectly happy to walk around picking up insects. Most prey is spotted from lookout perches, but it also scans for prey in flight, hovering when necessary. These hawks can gather into large flocks during winter and on migration. They are the most common raptors found in North and Central America. Their population has thrived after the arrival of the European settlers, whose destructive exploits accidentally created a habitat beneficial to them. However, they are regularly killed by flying into electric power lines and cars.

CRANE HAWK *Geranospiza caerulescens*
length 18 in (46 cm) wingspan 37 in (94 cm)

This is a strange-looking raptor with exceptionally long red legs. It can survive in a number of lowland habitats such as forest, mangroves, and wooded grassland and is found in South and Central America. It is a gray, long, slim, small-headed bird with a black-and-white barred tail and piercing red eyes. One race found in Mexico and Panama is black. The juvenile has a pale gray-blotched front. It has double-jointed legs, which it uses to clamber about trees, getting into all sorts of strange positions, wings spread, hanging upside down, as it pokes its head into holes and crevices in search of food. Its flexible legs are used to extract prey from tree crevices and holes. Its diet is varied and includes reptiles, frogs, and baby birds. It constructs a nest of sticks, lined with grass and small twigs and finished with leaves, in a tall tree.

COMMON BUZZARD *Buteo buteo*
length 18 in (46 cm) wingspan 48 in (122 cm)

This compact buzzard can vary in plumage from virtually all-dark individuals to white-and-brown blotched birds. Its wings are so broad that they make the tail appear quite short. Found across Asia, Europe, and Africa, it is usually one of the most common and widespread of raptors, and likes wooded open countryside. Some populations migrate, while others are resident. The latter call throughout the year and the characteristic mew calls are often heard first, before the bird is "clocked" high in the sky. The common buzzard can eat a wide variety of prey, ranging from mammals to earthworms and carrion. It will often hunt from perches, dropping onto the prey, but can also soar, glide, and hover in search of food and can collect earthworms on foot. Some will eat poisonous toads, removing the toxic skin on the back of the toad before swallowing. It can live for up to 26 years. Its nest is a large twiggy platform lined with leaves and constructed in a tall tree. It sometimes reuses abandoned raptor nests. As many as five eggs are laid and the young leave the nest some three months later. They are dependent on their parents for a further two months and are not ready to breed until three years old.

WESTERN HONEY BUZZARD *Pernis apivorus*

length 22 in (59 cm) wingspan 52 in (132 cm)

This secretive raptor has a head that superficially resembles that of a pigeon. It lives in lush woods with plenty of clearings. It spends the summer in Europe and western Siberia and heads south in winter to the warmer climate south of the Sahara Desert in Africa, when huge numbers can be seen passing over migration funnel points such as Gibraltar and the Bosphorus in Turkey. The adult is quite variable in plumage and appears slim, with long wings and tail. The head and bill are relatively small. Its talons, used for excavating bee and wasp nests, are fairly straight, and

its nostrils are just slits, to prevent soil blocking them as it digs. It may have immunity to the venom produced by these insects. It eats their larvae and will consume the adults once it has removed their sting by a nip from its bill. To protect it against any stings, the lores, the sides of the face near the bill, are covered with scaly feathers. The aerial display flight is distinctive, with the buzzard quivering its wings above its back at the top of each undulation. It constructs its nest from leafy twigs, often utilizing an old crow nest. It hides the nest with dead leaves. Breeding is timed so that the eggs hatch when bees are most plentiful.

● **KITES**
(13 species)

SNAIL KITE *Rostrhamus siciabilis*
length 17 in (43 cm) wingspan 46 in (117 cm)

The Snail Kite was formerly known as the Everglade Kite, a reflection of the fact that in the USA it is found only in Florida. It is, however, found throughout Central and South America and the Caribbean. Its range is governed by the distribution of Apple Snails (genus *Pomacea*), which it specializes in eating. Its bill is especially long and thin to allow easy extraction of the snail from its shell. In drought conditions, it will resort to crabs, turtles, and small mam-

mals. The male is dark all over, apart from a white band at the base of the tail. The female and immature birds are browner, with a spotted, paler front. Apple Snails live in marshy wetlands and consequently so do Snail Kites. In favorable areas, large numbers can gather, with up to 1,000 birds collecting at roost sites. It hunts for snails either from perches or by cruising with flapping flight, low over the marsh, and then plunging feet first to grab the snail in shallow water. It builds a stick nest in a tree often in loose colonies. When there is a plentiful supply of snails, one of the partners may depart before the young have flown the nest, leaving a single parent to raise the family. The deserter may go on to breed with a new mate.

BLACK-SHOULDERED KITE *Elanus caeruleus*

length 13 in (33 cm) wingspan 33 in (84 cm)

A small, ghostly-white, batlike kite, this raptor has a white underside, a gray back and tail, and a white face with piercing red eyes outlined in black. The immature bird is browner, with pale, scalloplike markings. It lives in fairly dry, open, grassy habitats, such as savannah, in Africa, Europe, and southern Asia and is very similar to the White-Tailed Kite found in the Americas. It hunts from perches for small birds, mammals, and reptiles, frequently cocking its tail up and down, and will at times also scan for prey in flight, often stopping to hover. One of this raptor's display flights is butterflylike; it flies slowly with stiff, exaggerated flaps. When there is plentiful food it can lay as many as six eggs, which is exceptional for a bird of prey. Outside the breeding season, as many as 500 birds can come together at communal roost sites in trees or reed beds.

BRAHMINY KITE *Haliastur indus*
length 23 in (58 cm) wingspan 47 in (119 cm)

This unique-looking kite has a white top half and a reddish-brown bottom half. Immature birds are streaked brown all over. It lives in woodland and farmland, from India throughout Southeast Asia to Australia, and is often found near coasts and marshy habitats. It can eat a wide variety of prey, including small mammals, birds, reptiles, amphibians, and fish, but also shellfish, crustaceans, and insects. It will consume carrion, too, including animals killed by vehicles. Potential food is spotted either from a perch or from the air during a soaring or quartering flight. The raptor grabs the prey with its feet and can pluck victims from trees or the surface of water in midflight. It will even steal food from other predators. Although this kite is common over much of its range, the population in Java has collapsed, possibly due to hunting, pesticide use, and tree felling. It needs trees or a suitable man-made structure in which to construct a stick nest.

57

BLACK KITE *Milvus migrans*
length 22 in (59 cm) wingspan 54 in (137 cm)

The Black Kite is similar to the Red Kite but is darker, stockier, has a shallower tail fork, and is found over a much wider range, including Australia, Southeast Asia, and Europe. It probably has the greatest population of any raptor, due to its ability to thrive in a wide range of habitats, exploiting a varied diet and grabbing any opportunity for a quick meal. It will steal food out of human hands, market stalls, and so on, as well as consuming carrion and other scraps. It hunts small mammals, birds, amphibians, insects and fish and will chase other bird species and force them to give up their food. The Black Kite is often found around urban areas,

particularly in Africa and Asia, and huge flocks can gather at roost sites, often in cities. Vast numbers can pass through migration bottlenecks. Up to 60,000 birds fly south over Gibraltar to Africa each autumn.

RED KITE *Milvus milvus*
length 26 in (66 cm) wingspan 62 in (157 cm)

This is a large, slender, long-winged kite with a reddish tail and underside. In flight it has a characteristically forked tail and pale patches on its wings. It lives in Europe and North Africa in open countryside with trees. Its diet is varied and includes birds and mammals and also carrion and other food debris, which it can scavenge from slaughterhouses, rubbish dumps, and roadside casualties. During the winter as many as 100 birds can gather at communal roost sites. Each bird constructs several nests in a large tree and can either use a different nest each year or the same one year after year. The nest is made of sticks with bits of discarded plastic thrown in and is lined with wool. The Red Kite can live for up to 26 years. Its numbers have been in decline for many reasons but mainly as a result of human activities. In the UK, reintroductions have been used to bolster the vulnerable population.

EAGLES

Eagles are birds of prey that hunt during the day. They have broad wings, a powerful bill, and talons that are used to grab their quarry. They have thick, short legs, which are feathered toward the top, a characteristic often referred to as trousers. The male has a similar plumage to the female, but she is generally larger. It takes several years for the young to mature to adults. They can live for up to 60 years and are top predators in the food chain. Eagles are divided into four groups according to their habits and body shapes: fish eagles, large forest eagles, snake eagles, and booted eagles. They vary in size and weight, the lightest weighing about one pound (0.45 kg) and the heaviest around 20 pounds (9 kg).

● FISH AND FISHING EAGLES

There are ten species that have a similar body structure and eat fish, but will also feed on carrion and will steal prey from other species, a practice known as kleptoparisitism. They usually hunt by scanning from a perch. When a suitable fish is detected they glide over and grab the prey with their feet.

WHITE-TAILED FISH EAGLE *Haliaeetus albicilla*
length 33 in (84 cm) wingspan 86 in (218 cm)

This is an awesomely huge eagle with such broad, long, rectangular wings that it has been a likened to a flying table. The adult is pale brown with a white, wedge-shaped tail and strong yellow feet and bill. Youngsters are brown all over. It lives by coasts, lakes, and rivers in northern Europe, Siberia, and Greenland. It eats mostly fish and birds, but many rely on carrion to survive the winter. It often steals food from other birds and has even been known to feed on human corpses. Occasionally these eagles will hunt in pairs, especially when they are preying on diving sea birds, which become exhausted more quickly under sustained attacks. At winter roost sites and where there is sufficient food, up to 100 birds can congregate. It builds a vast nest of sticks and branches, which over the years can become several feet thick. The nest is lined with softer material such as moss, grass, lichen, and wool, and is situated on a cliff ledge or large tree.

BALD EAGLE *Haliaeetus leucocephalus*
length 31 in (79 cm) wingspan 81 in (206 cm)

The Bald Eagle is the national symbol of the USA. The adult is brown with striking white head, neck, and tail. The feet, legs, and bill are yellow. In Old English, "balde" means "white," hence the name Bald Eagle. In young birds the plumage is brown all over. Its feathers were used in headdresses and armbands by Native American tribes. Although it is a large, strong, fish-eating eagle, it weighs less than most domestic cats. It can strike its prey with a force twice as powerful as that of a rifle bullet. Despite being classified as a fish eagle it will eat birds, mammals, reptiles, and carrion. It will steal fish, particularly from the osprey, and this has the added benefit of reducing the number of these competitors within the eagle's territory. It lives by coasts, lakes, and rivers in North America. Up to 200 can gather at the autumn spawning runs of salmon and there can be 1,000 birds at some winter roost sites. The aerie, or nest, is often used year after year, sometimes for decades. New material is added each year and they can become colossal structures, the largest having dimensions of 3.3 yards (3 m) wide and 5.5 yards (5 m) deep. Displays can include cartwheeling in the air, which is thought to be representative of a male tossing another from its territory. In Alaska, bounties were paid in the first half of the twentieth century for killing the Bald Eagle, and 150,000 were exterminated. Further huge losses occurred in the 1960s and '70s from poisoning by the pesticide DDT.

STELLER'S FISH EAGLE *Haliaeetus pelagicus*
length 37 in (94 cm) wingspan 84 in (213 cm)

This is even more massive than the White-Tailed Fish Eagle and has a huge, bulbous swollen yellow bill. The adult is brown with striking white shoulder patches, tail, and trousers. The immense wings bulge out so that they have the appearance of large paddles, and the tail is wedge-shaped. This eagle lives by the coast and large lakes in eastern Asia and hunts primarily for fish, but will eat carrion, especially in winter, as well as birds and mammals. Up to 2,000 birds, or one third of the entire world population, winter along the north coast of the Japanese island

of Hokkaido. The nest is a massive construction of sticks and branches on a tree or cliff ledge. Normally two eggs are laid and incubated for as long as 45 days. Usually only one of the young succeeds in fledging, after two and a half months. This raptor is classified as rare, with a total world population of only 7,500 birds. Threats to the species' survival include loss of forested habitats due to coastal development, logging, and hydroelectric power projects. Shooting and overfishing are also serious problems, and many nestlings die each year either by falling from the nest or if the whole nest collapses.

● **SNAKE AND SERPENT EAGLES**

There are 15 species in this group. The legs of these eagles are covered with scales that protect them against snake-bites, although their agility at avoiding the snake helps. Snake eagles will carry partly swallowed snakes headfirst to nestlings. The tail of the snake is left dangling from the raptor's bill. Serpent eagles are larger and less prone to attack, and carry their prey in their feet.

BATELEUR *Terathopius ecaudatus*

length 25 in (64 cm) wingspan 70 in (179 cm)

In flight, this is a bizarre-looking raptor. With its exceptionally short tail, it looks like a flying wing with a protruding head, and even when perched, its rear end appears to have been chopped off. It is dark with gray shoulders, and in females there is a gray wing panel. Its back and tail are orangey-red, while the bill and legs are a gaudy bright red. The underside of the wings are white bordered in black. It lives in the open grassland and savannah of Africa, south of the Sahara. Although classified as a snake eagle, it has a varied meaty diet, eating anything from a mouse to a small antelope, and will eat birds, insects, carrion, and some reptiles. It covers huge areas, spending many day-light hours searching for food, sometimes flying 310 miles (500 km) a day. With such long periods away, it is not surprising that a third of all nestlings fall victim to pre-dators. In display, its wings make a noise like a flapping sail, which can be heard over vast distances.

SHORT-TOED SNAKE EAGLE *Circaetus gallicus*
length 26 in (66 cm) wingspan 70 in (179 cm)

This eagle ranges in color from pale to fairly dark, with brown crescents and a solid, pale brown bill, although in some birds this is white. Its wings are long and broad, some having brown spots and bars on the undersides, while in others this area is nearly all white. Found in Europe and the Middle East in summer, this eagle winters in Africa. There is a resident population in India. It hunts for snakes and other meaty items over dry countryside and catches them by quartering at low levels. It will eat smaller prey in midair, killing it by crushing or ripping off the head. The mating display is a deep and undulating aerial display, often carrying a snake or twig in its bill. It will drop and catch the twig repeatedly, eventually passing the snake to its mate. The nestling period, the time between the young bird hatching and taking its first flight, is about a month.

67

● **LARGE EAGLES**

This group comprises four species of very large eagle that inhabit tropical rainforest.

HARPY EAGLE *Harpia harpyja*

length 38 in (97 cm) wingspan 74 in (188 cm)

The Harpy is a massive eagle that lives in lowland forest in South and Central America. It has huge rounded wings and a long broad tail to help it maneuver through the forest in pursuit of its main quarry, monkeys and sloths. It will also eat birds and reptiles. The adult has a gray head with a short black crest and a dark gray back and tail, which has black bars. It has a black chest bar but is otherwise pale underneath with some black barring. Juveniles are, unusually for raptors, paler all over. It has very solid legs with huge talons – the hind claw is a nasty 3 inches (7 cm). The females can weigh up to 20 pounds (9 kg). In some parts they are kept in captivity or killed for their feathers, which are used as decorative features in ceremonial costumes. It is a rare bird, other than in the Amazon, and breeds only every two to three years. The male of a pair delivers one item of prey per week to the incubating female and one item every three to five days to its nestling. The nestling period can be as long as five months. This raptor behaves aggressively toward intruders that get too close to the nest, which can include physically attacking humans. The Harpy Eagle Conservation Program liaises with Latin American authorities and organizations, including logging companies, to conserve forests and breeding sites. It has established a captive breeding and release program to restock areas where the bird has become locally extinct.

INDIAN BLACK EAGLE *Ictinaetus malayensis*
length 29 in (74 cm) wingspan 65 in (165 cm)

This largish, all-black eagle looks similar to a large kite. Its wings are broad, long, and slightly bulging so that superficially they resemble paddles. Young birds are paler and more streaked on the front. It lives in widespread scattered locations across Southeast Asia and although not globally threatened it is uncommon over much of its range. It prefers to live in hilly evergreen forest with clearings, but can survive in deciduous woods and secondary growth. It specializes in feeding on eggs and baby birds, but will also go for small mammals, reptiles, frogs, large insects, and, occasionally, bats. This raptor hunts by flying low over the canopy, seizing prey from the branches, and can also scramble around the branches, looking for nests. The structure of its foot is peculiar, with a short outer toe and less-curled talons, which are probably well designed for grabbing entire nests, including any eggs or young. Prey is often consumed on the wing. It nests in the top of a large tree, building a neat, well-hidden nest lined with green leaves. Stunning display flights include a headlong plunge with the wings folded into a tear shape.

GREAT PHILIPPINE EAGLE *Pithecophaga jefferyi*
length 37 in (94 cm) wingspan 76 in (193 cm)

This massive eagle is on the verge of extinction and is found only in the Philippines, where it is the national bird. There may be only just over 100 pairs left. The decline is due not only to rainforest clearance but also to trophy hunters and others capturing the birds to keep as pets. This raptor has short, broad, rounded wings and a longish tail. The underside is silvery white and the upper side is fawn-brown. The head is crowned with a dark shaggy crest, which can be raised, and the bill is chunky. The immature birds look similar to the adults. Although its alternative name is the Monkey-eating Eagle, its preferred diet is flying lemurs and palm civets. Perfectly designed to fly through the treetops, it snatches this prey off branches. It will also eat other mammals, including monkeys, birds and reptiles. It breeds only every couple of years, constructing a huge nest near the top of a very tall tree. The

single egg takes nearly two months to hatch and the young take up to half a year to fledge. The future of the species is dependent on the establishment of protected national parks in the few areas of suitable habitat that are left, and on reintroductions from captive breeding.

● **TRUE OR BOOTED (AQUILA) EAGLES**

GOLDEN EAGLE *Aquila chrysaetos*
length 31 in (79 cm) wingspan 81 in (206 cm)

This is a large brown eagle that has a golden patch on the back of the neck. Young birds have splashes of white in the wing and tail. It lives in remote areas, away from humans, across most of the northern hemisphere and can survive in a variety of habitats, ranging from arid deserts to the frozen north. It spends long periods perching on rocks or trees on the lookout for prey. Once it has spotted its victim it swoops

down at speeds of up to 150 miles an hour (257 km/h). Its favorite animals are medium-sized mammals such as rabbits and hares, or birds such as grouse. It will tackle birds the size of swans or cranes and, particularly in winter, it will eat carrion, including dead farm animals. In the drier habitats, reptiles are the preferred menu choice. This even includes tortoises, which the eagle will kill by dropping them in flight onto rocks. It prefers to nest on cliff ledges, constructing a huge aerie that is used year after year. The female lays two eggs, which take up to a month and a half to hatch. The young leave the nest after nearly three months and rely on their parents for a further four months. Golden Eagle feathers are worn as headdresses and arm bands by Native American tribes.

WEDGE-TAILED EAGLE *Aquila audax*

length 38 in (97 cm) wingspan 81 in (206 cm)

The plumage of this large eagle is superficially similar to that of the Golden Eagle, it being brown all over with a golden nape. But it has a more gangly shape, with longer, thinner wings, a long, wedge-shaped tail, and baggy trousers. It is a fairly sedentary creature but young birds will wander away from the nesting area and adults will move in drought conditions. It lives in Australia and can survive in a variety of habitats, including forest and savannah, but cannot find enough to eat on land that is farmed intensively. It can eat a wide variety of animals, varying in size from rabbits to kangaroos, and can catch birds up to the size of cranes. Several of these eagles can be attracted to a large carcass, where they will shove aside any smaller scavengers. Larger prey can be hunted down by small groups, including one record of 15 birds hunting a red kangaroo. The introduction of rabbits in Australia and forest clearance have resulted in healthier populations of the Wedge-Tailed Eagle. This is despite some persecution by farmers, who think, erroneously, that it preys on sheep and other farm animals. However, the race that lives in Tasmania is under threat, with perhaps only 160 birds left. They have been seen attacking hang-gliders or small aircraft, presumably because they perceive them as other eagle species that are encroaching on their territory.

● **HAWK EAGLES**

LONG-CRESTED EAGLE

Lophaetus occipitalis
length 21 in (53 cm) wingspan 48 in (122 cm)

The Long-Crested Eagle can be found in woodland, farmland, plantations, and savannah in Africa. It is a smallish, all-black eagle with a long, black, droopy crest, and long, broad, rounded wings that have white patches. In flight it often utters a high, drawn-out scream. Its favorite food is small rodents, but it will consume birds and reptiles and occasionally fish or fruit. Sometimes it will hang out for several days in an area good for hunting, such as one where there has been a recent grass fire, and can spend a long time on the lookout for prey from suitable perches. Once spotted, the quarry is swooped down on, seized with the eagle's talons and normally swallowed whole, as this raptor has a wide gape. Man tends not to hunt this species, appreciating its habit of eating rats and mice. The Long-Crested Eagle has adapted to surviving in new man-made habitats, such as small-scale farms and plantations.

BONELLI'S EAGLE *Hieraaetus fasciatus*
length 24 in (61 cm) wingspan 62 in (157 cm)

Bonelli's Eagle is found at scattered localities across Europe, North Africa, and the Middle East to Southeast Asia. It lives in alpine, wooded areas with gorges and cliffs for breeding. A smallish eagle with broad wings and long tail, the adult is brown above with a white patch on the back, and pale cinnamon coloring below with black streaks. Juveniles are buff. Its diet consists of medium-sized birds and mammals. In Europe, its favorite food is rabbit and partridge, while in India it will take chickens and pigeons. An extremely agile flier, it launches attacks from a perch and seizes the prey from the ground. However, it can also take birds in midair and sometimes pairs will hunt together. It usually builds its large nest, made of stick and lined with leaves, on a cliff ledge or sometimes in a tall tree. The population of this species has declined since the 1950s due to human persecution and the incidence of young birds hitting power lines.

VERREAUX'S EAGLE *Aquila verreauxii*

length 33 in (84 cm) wingspan 79 in (201 cm)

The all-black Verreaux's Eagle has a pale patch in each wing and a distinctive white rump and white "V" on the back. Its wings appear paddle-shaped, being bulged and nipped in at the base. The immature bird is dark brown with pale-blotched plumage. It is found in Africa and a small area of the Middle East. It inhabits dry, rocky, mountainous areas. It eats mostly rock hyraxes and some other mammals, birds, and tortoises, catching them with a surprise attack as it flies out from behind rocks or from outside the victim's line of sight. These eagles often hunt in pairs, one distracting the prey while the other appears suddenly from behind. They will even knock the intended prey off a cliff. A pair of adults and one young bird can eat up to 400 hyrax in the breeding season. The nestling period is 95-130 days.

LITTLE EAGLE *Hieraaetus morphnoides*
length 18 in (46 cm) wingspan 47 in (119 cm)

This is a small, chunky eagle with a little crest. The adult is dark brown above and pale underneath, with some black streaking on the breast. Found in Australia and New Guinea in open woodland and scrub, it eats mainly mammals but also birds, reptiles, insects, and carrion. Prey is normally spotted from the air by systematic quartering of suitable habitat or by soaring high on thermals and then swooping onto the quarry. The Little Eagle will often be seen hanging in the wind with its tail fanned as it zeroes in on its prey. It will also hunt from perches, plunging onto the prey feetfirst, with wings raised. Its nest is a bulky structure constructed with sticks and lined with green leaves in a tall tree. It will often use an old raptor nest. Like the Wedge-Tailed Eagle, its numbers in parts of Australia have increased as a direct result of forest clearance and the introduction of rabbits.

BOOTED EAGLE *Hieraaetus pennatus*
length 18 in (46 cm) wingspan 56 in (142 cm)

This is a small, "buteo"-sized eagle that comes in two forms, pale and dark. The latter is dark brown all over, while the pale form is light brown above and cream below. Both have a pale rump and pale upper wing markings. Head-on, two conspicuous white "headlights" are visible at the base of the wings. The immature bird is very like the adult pale form. Found in areas of forest and open woodland in Europe, Africa, and the Middle East, it eats mostly reptiles and mammals, and swarming insects in tropical regions. It hunts mainly in flight and from up high it can drop in stages, hanging in the wind as it zeroes in on its prey, before finally bringing its feet forward to grasp the victim. The aerial display includes a steep dive on closed wing before rising again. This can be continued for half an hour with very little loss of height.

● **HARRIERS**

Harriers have a distinctive flight, with their long wings and broad secondaries held up in a "V" shape. They have a weak bill and their legs are thin and long. Their excellent hearing is improved by a large facial ruff and large ear openings, which are useful for locating prey in thick cover.

NORTHERN MARSH HARRIER *Circus aeruginosus*
length 19 in (48 cm) wingspan 51 in (130 cm)

This harrier lives in and around marshy habitats, but it will hunt over other types of open countryside, including farmland. The male has silvery-white, black, and brown plumage. The female and young are brown with cream face markings. It is relatively bulky and, in common with most harriers, it glides and soars on "V"-shaped wings. It is found across Europe, Siberia, and Asia, with some populations wintering in Africa. Although it eats a similar diet to other harrier species, it will eat carrion more readily and can hover when trying to locate prey. The male has a spectacular, seemingly out-of-control aerial display, which includes twisting, somer-saulting, loops, rolls, and spinning while plummeting from up high. During the breeding season the male regularly passes prey to his mate, in flight, by dropping the food into her talons, which she receives in midflight by rolling onto her back. The male will often pair with more than one female during the breeding season. In these situations the top female is fed more frequently by him than are the other one to two females and thus is more likely to survive and successfully rear chicks.

NORTHERN HARRIER *Circus hudsonius*

length 18 in (46 cm) wingspan 43 in (109 cm)

The only harrier species to breed in North America, the Northern Harrier used to be called the Marsh Hawk. In winter, some migrate as far south as northern South America. The male is silvery-gray and white, with black wing tips. The female is browner, while the immature is rusty looking. All have a white rump. It hunts by quartering back and forth low over open countryside such as wetland and farmland on the lookout for small mammals, birds, reptiles, and amphibians. Having detected its prey, it can turn and drop rapidly onto it. It may kill wildfowl by drowning them. It breeds in marshy areas, constructing a platform of grasses and reed mixed with other vegetation. The male can mate with up to three females and performs an impressive roller-coaster display flight to attract them. The loss of its marshland habitat has resulted in a reduction in population of this harrier. Shooting and the indiscriminate use of pesticides have taken their toll.

PIED HARRIER *Circus melanoleucus*

length 18 in (46 cm) wingspan 46 in (117 cm)

This harrier winters in the paddies and marshes of Southeast Asia and summers in the steppe and bogs of eastern Siberia. The male is distinctive, its black head, shoulders, breast, and wing tips contrasting with its silvery white underparts and forewing. The female is gray and brown above and lighter below, with a small white rump. It hunts by quartering suitable habitat on buoyant wings. It eats mostly small mammals, amphibians, reptiles and insects. Although it usually hunts alone, loose flocks can gather when there is a concentration of prey in one area. It joins other harriers at safe roost sites. The nest is merely a flat pad of grass or reeds, usually built on wet ground hidden by marshy vegetation. The female lays up to five eggs, one every other day. Since she starts incubating the first egg as soon as it is laid, the young hatch at different times, resulting in different-sized young in the nest. Only if food is in plentiful supply will they all survive.

87

● **OSPREY** *Pandion haliaetus*
length 23 in (58 cm) wingspan 59 in (150 cm)
This is a truly cosmopolitan species
found in every continent except the
Arctic regions. It breeds in the
northern hemisphere and Australia and
winters mainly in the southern hemisphere.
The osprey is a largish, long-winged hawk, which
is basically brown above and white below. It has beady
yellow eye and a broad, dark face band. It lives near salt-
or freshwater and feeds almost entirely on fish, usually
catching them by circling and hovering 30 to 100 feet
(10–30 m) above the surface of the water and then plunge-
diving, feet first, into the water. It has several features that
are just perfect for grasping slimy and wriggling fish: the
fourth toe can be moved to the back of its foot so that two
toes face forward and two backward; the soles of its feet
are spiny; and the claws are exceptionally curled. On rare
occasions, an osprey has been known to select such a large
fish that it has been dragged under and drowned. This
raptor builds a substantial nest out of small branches. The
nest is often used year after year, with new material being
added each year. Numbers declined where the pesticide
DDT was used in the 1950s. There has since been a
population recovery, achieved partly by introducing
young ospreys into areas where they had died out.

● **SECRETARY BIRD** *Sagittarius serpentarius*
length 54 in (137 cm) wingspan 78 in (120 cm)
Superficially, this unique-looking raptor bears more resemblance to a stork. With its long legs and neck it is about half the height of a human. Its plumage is gray all over, although somewhat paler on the underside, with long black feathers at the back of the head and a patch of orangey-red bare skin around the face. Most distinctive are the long central tail feathers. The fronts of the legs are covered in tough scales, which may protect it when walking through grassland, or from struggling prey. The Secretary Bird lives exclusively in Africa, in the grasslands and savannah south of the Sahara. It eats prey up to the size of hares and its diet includes insects, mice, and snakes. It

locates them by patrolling suitable habitats on foot and can travel up to 13 miles (21 km) a day. A nomadic bird, it moves to new areas in response to fluctuations in the numbers of prey. Victims are dispatched with fast kicks from its strongly webbed front toes. It has a wide gape and often swallows prey whole, although it pulls apart larger animals with its bill while holding down the quarry with its foot. It will often stash prey for eating later. It has not been widely persecuted by man, who has looked favorably on its diet of mice and snakes. Often seen in pairs, it nests and roosts on acacia trees. The young are fed initially on a partially digested soup of insects, and the adult bird can deliver water to its nestlings by trickling it into the chick's bill.

● FALCONIFORMES
15 species

CARACARAS
These raptors are distinguishable from hawks in flight as their wings are bent back at the wrist. They have fairly long, rounded wings. Most are scavengers feeding on a wide variety of carrion and smallish prey. The Guadalupe Caracara, which lived on Guadalope Island off Baja, Mexico, has been extinct since the nineteenth century. Amazingly, this is the only bird of prey known to have become extinct since 1600.

CRESTED CARACARA *Caracara planus*
length 23 in (58 cm) wingspan 47 in (119 cm)
Its striking black-and-white plumage, black crown with a short crest, silver bill, bare red face, and yellow feet and legs make this a distinctive species. In flight the dark wings and body contrast with the black-and-white barred primaries and tail. The largest of the caracaras, it lives in grassland and open woodland in South and Central America, just reaching some of the southern US. Although it will eat a lot of carrion, it will attack small prey, especially if they happen to be injured or immobile, and will steal food from other species, such as hawks and pelicans, pursuing them, in flight, until they regurgitate and/or drop their last meal. The caracara will fly along roads looking for corpses and will even follow cars or trains, since it has learned that passengers sometimes throw out scraps. It builds an untidy nest of sticks on top of a cactus, tree, or even on the ground.

● **FOREST FALCONS**

As their name suggests, these birds live in forested areas and have shorter, rounded wings and longer tails than true falcons, allowing them to maneuver through trees with ease.

COLLARED FOREST FALCON

Micra semitorquatus
length 20 in (51 cm) wingspan 31 in (79 cm)
This large, slender forest falcon comes in three forms, with white, buff, or black undersides. All have dark upper sides, pale bars on the tail, and barred underwings. The buff and

white forms have a pale collar. This raptor is found in South and Central America, occasionally reaching as far north as Texas. Throughout much of its range it is uncommon, but this may be a reflection of its secretive habits. It lives in forested areas and hunts in the foliage, moving from perch to perch on the lookout for mammals, birds such as toucans, reptiles and larger insects. It will even run though the understory in attempts to catch prey. Its presence can be detected by its laughlike call, which is usually uttered from a high perch, particularly at dawn and dusk. The breeding biology of this falcon is poorly understood, but it nests in a multi-entrance hollow in trees, and sometimes in ruined buildings.

AFRICAN PYGMY-FALCON

Polihierax semitorquatus
length 8 in (20 cm) wingspan 15 in (38 cm)

A miniature, pretty species, the African Pygmy-Falcon has a distinctive, undulating flight. It has a white underside with gray and black wings, which are barred on the underside. The male is gray above and the female has a chestnut back. Both have white faces. The feet and cere are red. It lives in Africa, favoring dry savannah, and its distribution mirrors that of the Weaver species, in whose nests it breeds and roosts. Couples, and sometimes the entire family, will roost in the same nest chamber or neighboring ones. During cold winter periods it can spend up to 15 hours a day in the Weaver's nest and can become somewhat hypothermic. It perches in trees, wagging its tail when excited and bobbing its head just before takeoff. It can turn its head right around in search for its prey, insects and lizards, which it catches by diving onto them.

LAUGHING FALCON *Herpetotheres cachinnans*
length 19 in (48 cm) wingspan 33 in (84 cm)

Inhabiting woody areas of South and Central America, the Laughing Falcon avoids dense primary rainforest. It has a buff underside, head, and neck with a striking broad black mask. The relatively short wings and back are dark gray-brown and the relatively long tail is barred. It calls much more regularly than most birds of prey and, as its name suggests, it has a distinctive laughing call. It can also utter a call that sounds reminiscent of a child shouting and yet another, "wah"-sounding call is repeated with increasing pitch and volume for several minutes. Pairs will sometimes duet, mostly at dawn and dusk but also during the night. Its favorite food is snakes, even large poisonous ones. It spots them from favored perches that give good all-round viewing, often sitting patiently for long stretches, with head slightly bowed. It nests in trees, occasionally using an old raptor nest, or sometimes in a hole in a cliff. This species is quite uncommon over most of its range.

97

SPOT-WINGED FALCONET

Spiziapteryx circumcinctus
length 11 in (28 cm) wingspan 20 in (51 cm)

This tiny, funny-looking raptor is dark above and pale with dark streaks below. The black wings have white speckles and the rump is white. Unusually for falcons, the immature birds look like the adults. The bill is "untoothed" and the feet have hexagonal scales, which indicate that it is a primitive species in evolutionary terms. Found in savannah and dry, scrubby areas of southern South America, it eats large insects, small mammals, and birds, including adult and young Monk Parakeets. During the breeding season it commandeers another suitable bird's nest by either enlarging the entrance hole or partially demolishing the roof to provide a nesting platform. Bizarrely, it will roost in a Monk Parakeet nest even when it is in use. How well the Monk Parakeet and its young sleep next to an intruder that may well end up eating them is not known!

● **TYPICAL FALCONS**

This family contains 45 species, which all have long pointed wings, strong hooked bills, and sharp, curved talons. They are brilliant at flying and their sight is remarkable. They often have bright yellow legs, orbital ring, and cere. The short bill and associated muscles are designed for killing prey by biting. Their bills are designed for slicing through flesh, having "tomial" teeth in the upper mandible and corresponding notches in the lower. Most species have dark malar stripes down from the front part of the eyes, which may reduce sun glare. They often bob their head when perched, and many species keep a larder of prey from which they can feed later.

SEYCHELLES KESTREL *Falco araea*

length 9 in (23 cm) wingspan 18 in (46 cm)

This tiny, beautiful falcon has peachy-salmon underparts, a dirty-gray head and a rusty back with black spots. Unusually for a kestrel, the female's plumage is very similar to the male's. Young birds have a spotty front. It is the only bird of prey that lives in the Seychelles, mainly on the largest island, Mahe, but also on some of the smaller islands, including Praslin, where it was reintroduced in 1977. Originally inhabiting the primary forest that grew on the island, it now lives in secondary growth and has adapted to survive in man-made, open habitats such as golf courses. It eats mostly lizards. Hunting from a perch, it swoops down and grabs the prey. It can nest in a variety of locations, including building ledges or disused Common Myna nests, but prefers holes in a rock face over 200 yards (or meters) above sea level.

COMMON KESTREL *Falco tinnunculus*
length 9 in (23 cm) wingspan 18 in (46 cm)

This is one of the most common raptors in its range and is found across Europe, the Middle East, Asia, and Africa. The male has a gray head and tail with a rusty-spotted brown back. The underside is lighter with dark spots. The female is browner on the upper side and blotchier on the underside. It can survive in a variety of open and woody habitats, such as grassland, semi-desert, farmland and even built-up areas. Having adapted to many man-made changes to the environment, it will often nest in church towers or bridges and has become a familiar sight floating over roadside borders. By hovering or perching it can locate prey below, detecting urine trails excreted by small rodents such as voles. It will also eat birds, reptiles, and insects. It can nest on cliff ledges, in tree holes, and in abandoned crow nests. The female lays up to seven eggs and can live for up to 16 years.

AMERICAN KESTREL *Falco sparverius*
length 9 in (23 cm) wingspan 22 in (56 cm)

The American Kestrel is a small, colorfully marked falcon. The male has black, blue-gray, white, and rufous coloring. The female looks duller. It is the most common and wide-spread falcon of its range, from the tip of South America to the northern latitudes of Canada and Alaska. It can live in a wide variety of habitats, including farmland and urban areas. Although it prefers to hunt from perches, it can hover, especially in windy conditions, and eats insects, small mammals, and reptiles. It can nest in old crow nests or by simply laying the eggs into the depression at the top of a royal palm. It will also nest in cavities, such as old woodpecker holes, and its use of artificial nest boxes has helped to repopulate some areas, such as in Florida, where it had declined in numbers. In many areas its population is increasing, and it is one of the most common falcons in the New World.

ELEONORA'S FALCON *Falco eleonorae*
length 15 in (38 cm) wingspan 37 in (94 cm)

There are two forms of this largish, sleek falcon, pale and dark. Both have dark upper sides, but the pale form has a buff underside with black chevrons. The head appears hooded, with a black mustachelike streak. It breeds on cliff edges, mainly on remote Mediterranean islands and islets situated on the migration route of smaller birds. The hatching of its young coincides with the arrival of these small birds, when they are making their way south for winter. The falcon hunts these migrants, often plucking them out of midair offshore and returning to feed them to its young. Sometimes many will form a loose, hovering flock, picking off tired migrants as they arrive. Crevices and holes in cliffs, and on the ground, serve as nests, often in loose colonies where they can be as close as just a few yards apart. The adult falcon eats mainly insects and will extend its hunt to mainland areas. It winters on Madagascar, where it likes open woodland and wetlands.

SOOTY FALCON *Falco concolor*

length 14 in (32-37 cm) wingspan 32 in (75-88 cm)

This species has some similarities to the Eleonora's Falcon. It is an all-dark raptor with yellow feet, orbital ring, and cere. Young birds look similar to the pale form of Eleonora's Falcon but are even lighter in color. It breeds in the desert and coastal areas of northeast Africa and the Middle East, sometimes in loose colonies of up to 100 pairs. The nest is merely a scrape in a hollow in rocks, coral, or on a cliff edge. The female lays up to four eggs, which take about a month to hatch. It winters in Madagascar and the adjoining African coast. Like the Eleonora's Falcon, it feeds its young on small autumn-migrant birds, and hatching coincides with the greatest influx of these small birds. The adult eats mainly insects, especially in its winter quarters. It can be seen hunting with the Eleonora's Falcon, and usually hunts at dawn and dusk, often in pairs.

MERLIN *Falco columbarius*
length 11 in (28 cm) wingspan 25 in (64 cm)

The Merlin is a small falcon found in open habitats such as moor and tundra right across the northern hemisphere. The male has a gray-blue back and streaky, rusty front. The female is browner. It eats mostly small, ground-nesting birds and some mammals, reptiles, and insects. Pairs will often hunt together and as many as eight have been seen at one time hunting insects. It usually launches its attack from a perch, skimming low over the ground and grabbing its victim in midair. Very occasionally it will hover. The Merlin usually either nests in old raptor or crow nests or simply makes a scrape on the ground, especially if there are few ground predators. However, it will attack intruders, including humans. The female lays up to six eggs, which take about a month to hatch, the male helping in incubation for up to a fifth of the time. Most Merlins migrate south of their breeding range in winter.

NORTHERN HOBBY *Falco subbuteo*

length 12 in (30 cm) wingspan 30 in (76 cm)

This slim falcon lives in open countryside containing a few trees throughout Europe and Asia and winters in southern Africa, India, and Southeast Asia. It is dark above, with a dark hood, partly white cheeks, and a dark spotted front, and sports rufous-orange trousers and under-tail coverts. In young birds these appear washed out. Its preferred diet is insects such as dragonflies and birds. Exceptional agility and sharp maneuverability enable it to catch and devour insects on the wing. Quite large, loose flocks can gather at a particularly good feeding area. It will patrol the roost sites or colonies of its prey species and is attracted to bush fires in search of easy pickings. This raptor has even been seen to follow agricultural vehicles in the hope that potential prey will be flushed out. During nesting and before undertaking the return journey for winter, it eats proportionately more birds, especially swallows, martins, and swifts, which presumably provide greater energy during those more exhausting times. It nests in disused crow nests in trees, laying up to four eggs, which take about a month to hatch.

LANNER FALCON *Falco biarmicus*
length 17 in (43 cm) wingspan 40 in (102 cm)

This medium-sized falcon has a distinctive rufous cap, dark upper parts and a pale underside with dark spots. Young birds are darker on the underside. It lives in Africa, the Middle East, and southern Europe and occupies a variety of dry, mainly open habitats, although it can live in wooded areas and has adapted to some urban districts in Africa. This raptor eats mainly birds, mammals, and reptiles. It often hunts where birds flock, such as at drinking holes or colonial nesting sites. It will even go for domestic chickens, if available, and will follow native hunters, grabbing any prey they may flush out. Lanner Falcons often hunt in pairs, although as many as 20 have been seen together when their prey species is concentrated. They will sometimes hide their prey for consumption later. The nest is a scrape on cliff ledges or on the ground and the raptor can utilize disused bird nests in trees or even on electricity towers.

SAKER FALCON *Falco cherrug*
length 20 in (51 cm) wingspan 44 in (112 cm)

Found in scattered localities across Africa, southeast Europe, the Middle East, and Asia, this is a large, bulky falcon. It is brown above and pale below, with brown chevron markings. It lives in wild open places, especially those with mountains and gorges, and nests in old crow nests or on cliff ledges. It eats mainly mammals and some birds, reptiles and insects, hunting either from perches or by scanning in flight from a height of about 22 yards (20 meters). It will stoop from a great height on birds and even make "mock" stoops on large mammals, including humans. It can catch birds up to the bulk of a bustard, which is the size of a large chicken. The Saker Falcon nests on cliff edges or in disused raptor or crow nests, although in some areas it prefers to nest on electricity towers, which it also uses as a perch from which to hunt. Some pressure is put on this falcon's population by falconers, the females and chicks being particularly highly prized among particular Arabic falconers, who use them to hunt for Houbara Bustards in the Middle East and even in North Africa.

GYR *Falco rusticolus*
length 22 in (59 cm) wingspan 46 in (117 cm)

This is the largest falcon that breeds in the Arctic regions. Many birds, especially the young, migrate southward in winter to avoid the big freeze. The color of the plumage varies between different populations, but there are three main forms, white, gray, and blackish-brown. The first is startlingly white with black chevrons on the wings and back, while the two other forms are progressively darker. The Gyr is the mascot for the United States Air Force Academy. It lives by coasts, lakes, or rivers with cliffs nearby, on which it can nest, although it will sometimes use the old nest of a raven or another raptor. Dramatic aerial display flights include steep dives and climbs and a flightline that forms a figure of eight when it passes over the aerie. It eats mostly birds such as grouse, waders, and ducks, with the occasional mammal thrown in, such as hares and lemmings. The Gyr's usual hunting technique is to fly fast and low, hugging the ground, and then, before the coup de grace, to rise and stoop onto the prey. Although not globally threatened, as many as 1,000 a year are taken by Siberian trappers, as well as an unknown number captured for falconers.

PEREGRINE FALCON *Falco peregrinus*
length 17 in (43 cm) wingspan 40 in (102 cm)

This species is famous for being the fastest animal in the world, with diving stoops recorded at speeds of 112 miles per hour (180 km/h). Although this large falcon is found all over the world and is the most naturally widespread of any bird species, it is far from the most common. The population declined in many areas due to pesticide use in the 1960s and '70s, DDT contamination causing the eggshells to thin so that breeding success declined. In some regions, such as the eastern USA, the Peregrine Falcon was completely wiped out, but reintroduction programs have helped to repopulate these areas. A short-tailed, stocky-looking falcon, its plumage varies across its range but is basically dark above and lighter underneath with dark barring and a dark head hood. Immature birds are browner. It can survive in a wide variety of habitats, from

deserts to tropical forests to Arctic tundra. Nesting sites are usually out of reach on cliff ledges, tall trees, or even high, man-made structures, but some nest on the ground. Its preferred diet is other bird species, which are killed in flight after a spectacular stoop, although it will also consume the occasional mammal, reptile, and even insects.

PRAIRIE FALCON *Falcon mexicanus*
length 17 in (43 cm) wingspan 40 in (102 cm)

The Prairie Falcon is dark brown above with a pale underside with dark brown streaks. In flight, it has dark "armpits" and a dark bar along the center of the underwing. It is found in the western USA and is more common in the northern part of its range. Avoiding urban and forested areas, it lives in dry uplands and foothills and, as its name suggests, it hunts over prairies and grassland. It eats small mammals, birds and reptiles, and has a penchant for ground squirrels. This raptor's usual hunting technique is to cruise at moderate heights and, once the prey is spotted, to swoop down, grabbing the victim with its talons. It can even hover if required. It generally nests in holes in cliffs or cliff ledges or, occasionally, nests on buildings or electricity towers, and will sometimes make use of an old raven nest in a tall tree. Although not globally threatened, its total world population is only about 12,000 birds. Some are taken for use in falconry.

RED-HEADED OR RED-NECKED FALCON

Falco chicquera

length 13 in (33 cm) wingspan 25 in (64 cm)

This is a beautiful, slim falcon that lives in Africa and India. It has a rufous head and nape, white cheeks and salmon-pink breast, gray-and-black wings and tail, and is lightly barred on the underside. Hunting mostly at dawn and dusk, primarily for other species of bird, it often launches its attack from a perch hidden by vegetation. It can even fly straight upward, if necessary, and is not concerned about diving into foliage in pursuit of its quarry. This raptor often hunts in pairs, with both birds later sharing any kill, and has been recorded several times teaming up with the Gabar Goshawk in pursuit of prey. It breeds quite late in the dry season, when hunting is easiest. This is because there are many young birds around and the vegetation has dried out, so they are easier to spot. The Red-Headed Falcon often nests in old crow or raptor nests.

113

ORDER: STRIGIFORMES - OWLS

Owls are divided into two families, barn owls (Tytonidae) and the much larger group, typical owls (Strigidae). These raptors hunt their prey mainly at night. They have strong, hooked bills and sharp hooked talons. Their plumage is dense with a soft surface and their wings are large compared to body size, both characteristics allowing a silent flight and a surprise attack on their prey. They have a large head, often with facial disc, ruff, and ear tufts. The ruff helps enormously in hearing. Although the ear tufts are referred to as "ears," they are actually feathers. An owl's real ears are on the side of its head, covered by feathers. The ear openings in the skull of many owl species are at different heights, which allows them to pinpoint noises made by their prey. Their eyes are relatively large, some species having eyes that are larger than those of humans. The eyes are not quite directed fully forward, which would allow the maximum degree of binocular vision, but diverge slightly, giving a more extensive field of view. Bobbing and moving its head from side to side enables the owl to measure distances very accurately, and it can turn its head up to 270 degrees. The sexes are similar, although the female is often slightly larger. Plumage is often cryptic so that the raptor can roost in the day, concealed by its camouflage. If discovered, though, owls will be noisily mobbed by other birds. They nest in cavities, disused nests, or on the ground, laying white, rounded eggs. Many will happily breed in artificial nest boxes. Adults carry food in their bills to their young. Diurnal birds of prey carry the food in their talons. After eating, they produce pellets, which are regurgitated from their mouths and consist of fur, bone, and other indigestible material. Males hunt and provide for the female during incubation.

BARN OWLS AND BAY OWLS

This family includes 14 different species of barn owl and two species of bay owl. They all have an obvious heart-shaped facial ruff, long legs, and elongated bill, and most have a sawlike middle claw.

BARN OWLS

Members of the barn owl family have a characteristic threat display. The owl will bow forward, toward the intruder, open its wings and tilt them forward, spreading its tail at the same time. It then swings or nods its head and makes hissing noises and snaps with its bill. If that is not enough to deter any would-be intruder, it can attack with its talons and even spurt droppings at the perceived threat. Young birds in the nest will do this if provoked. The owl can also lie on its back with its eyes shut pretending to be dead in the hope that any predator will lose interest in eating it.

BARN OWL *Tyto alba*

length 16 in (41 cm) wingspan 35 in (89 cm)

This is a cosmopolitan species that is found throughout the world and is one of the most widely distributed land birds. Different populations of Barn Owl show many plumage variations. Birds from the UK appear ghostly white on the underside with yellow and blue-gray markings on the back, while other populations may have an orange front and more blue-gray on the back. Capable of survival in a variety of open habitats, it will often roost and breed in agricultural buildings – including barns! It can nest in trees, on cliffs, and even on the ground. Using the differences in sound received by its two asymmetrically positioned ear openings, it is able to locate its favorite prey, small mammals, in complete darkness. The total population of the Barn Owl fluctuates in response to the changing numbers of its prey species. It has a scary, screeching call. If it feels alarmed it will shut its eyes and draw itself upright, wrapping its wings closely around its body, thus concealing its pale front plumage. To intimidate any potential predators it can make itself as big as possible by bowing forward, toward the intruder, and spreading its wings, which are then tilted forward with tail spread and raised. To add to the effect it sways its body from side to side, hissing and snapping its bill. If that is not enough it will occasionally make sudden forward lunges, while glaring at the intruder. Its final defense is to act dead by closing its eyes and lying on its back.

GREATER SOOTY OWL *Tyto tenebricosa*
length 17 in (43 cm) wingspan 35 in (89 cm)

This is one of the darkest owls in the world, being sooty-black all over, apart from a smattering of small silver spots and a paler facial disc. Its tail is remarkably short, giving the bird a top-heavy appearance. It can produce a bizarre ear-piercing shriek that sounds like a dropping bomb. It lives in the wet forests of Australia and New Guinea, where it preys mostly on mammals ranging in size from opossums to mice. It often hunts in pairs, the male flying through the forest canopy with the female behind and below him, and grabs its prey in flight or by launching attacks from a perch. It nests in a cavity in a tree or high up in large caves. Some sites can be used for years; one well-studied nest site in a cave has been found to have been occupied for 10,000 years, based on an analysis of the debris below the nest, which included remains of extinct species.

ORIENTAL OR ASIAN BAY OWL *Phodilus badius*

length 11 in (28 cm) wingspan 20 in (51cm)

This small owl lives in the forests of Southeast Asia, but is rare over much of its range. It has a square-shaped facial disc and protruding, short ear tufts. Adults have a chestnut back and spotted front. Calls include one uttered during the breeding season that sounds like several cats fighting. It eats a variety of prey, from insects to small mammals, and especially likes beetles and flowerpeckers (birds). It has short, rounded wings, good for maneuvering through the forest in pursuit of prey, which it can catch on the wing. It will often perch sideways on vertical saplings, behavior that has only been observed in one other species of owl. It lays between two and five eggs in an unlined hollow in a tree, but the incubation period and other breeding biology is unknown. The only other bay owl is the Congo Bay Owl, which was not discovered until 1951.

119

STRIGIDAE FAMILY – TYPICAL OWLS

This is the largest family of owls, with 189 species ranging in size: the Elf Owl, which weighs in at just under a pound (40 g) to the 9 lb (4 kg) Eurasian Eagle Owl. They all have a round facial disc and a more rounded head than barn owls, as well as other morphological differences. The plumage of typical owls is often cryptic, or camouflaged. The family is broken down into three subfamilies and six tribes.

● SCOPS OWLS AND SCREECH OWLS
68 species

SCOPS OWL *Otus scops*
length 8 in (20 cm) wingspan 23 in (58 cm)

This small owl comes in two forms, one gray-brown and the other rufous-brown. It has a pale gray facial disc with small ear tufts, the front has dark streaks and the back has white blobs. A mostly migratory bird, it spends the warm summer months across Europe to western Siberia and winters in Africa. It breeds in somewhat open woodland, including town parks. It eats small prey such as insects and earthworms, but will also tackle small mammals and birds. It prefers to pounce on prey from perches, grabbing the victim with its talons, and can catch moths in midair and get hold of small quarry with its bill. If disturbed at roost in the day, it will adopt a sleek, upright pose and can also fold one of its wings across its front. This behavior and its bark-like plumage make it look like a tree stump. It has become more restricted in range due to loss of habitat and industrialized farming practices that has reduced the population of large insects.

EASTERN SCREECH OWL *Otus asio*

length 9 in (23 cm) wingspan 21 in (53 cm)

One of the best-known owls in eastern North America, this species is found in woods and urban gardens. It has a western counterpart called the Western Screech Owl. It is a small tufted owl that ranges in color from reddish-brown to gray. It has an undulating flight and a familiar whinnying call, but not a screech, as its name would suggest. This raptor's exceptionally varied diet includes small birds, mammals, and aquatic invertebrates. It can even catch fish, feet first, in shallow water. It normally hunts from perches, swooping down onto unsuspecting victims. It nests in rotted or storm-damaged trees or in disused woodpecker nest holes and will also use nest boxes provided by man. The female can lay up to seven eggs. During the day, it will often sit in the entrance hole of its roost site. This species is not under threat, and exploits man-made suburban habitats unusually well.

● EAGLE OWLS AND ALLIES
25 species

EURASIAN EAGLE OWL *Bubo bubo*
length 26 in (66 cm) wingspan 68 in (173 cm)

This is a massive brown owl with protruding ear tufts and intense red-orange eyes. It has a deep, booming, two-note call, which has given rise to local names such as "Buho" in Spain. Even its Latin name mimics the sound of its call. It usually lives in remote habitats away from humans, or in places inaccessible to them, such as rocky gorges. Hunting over open countryside, including farmland and even gar-

bage dumps, it can consume large prey up to the size of a hare or heron. Its diet varies, depending on the relative abundance of its prey. It hunts mostly from perches or by searching in flight and usually nests on the ground, on a cliff ledge or in an old tree. The female lays two to four eggs, which are incubated for just over a month. The young take up to six months before they become completely independent of their parents. Cannibalism has been witnessed among this species, where one of the parents or older siblings eats the youngest baby. The Eagle Owl is uncommon or rare over much of its range but is not globally threatened. Human persecution in the nineteenth century resulted in a decrease in the population in parts of its range, but more recent protection and some reintroductions have helped.

SNOWY OWL *Nyctea scandiaca*
length 24 in (61 cm) wingspan 60 in (152 cm)

The male of this species is a large, ghostly white owl with a rounded head and no ear tufts. The female is also white but has black spots. It is one of the few species of owl in which the sexes are identifiable in the field. It has dense feathering on its legs and toes to help it survive in Arctic regions. Many migrate south in winter to avoid the freeze and the resulting shortage in food supply, such as lemmings, which are among its favorite foods. It breeds in the open tundra but can survive in winter hunting over grasslands and marshes. It often flies about during the day. It nests on the ground on a raised site, allowing good views of the sur-

rounding terrain so that any potential predators are easily spotted. Intruders can be distracted by one of the adults pretending to be injured, and award-winning performances can lure the danger away from the nest. The female scrapes a simple depression for a nest and lines it with moss, grass, and lichen. In good lemming years the female can lay as many as 11 eggs, but in poor lemming years it may not breed at all.

BUFFY FISH OWL *Ketupa ketupa*
length 18 in (46 cm) wingspan 44 in (112 cm)

This is the smallest of the fish-eating owls known as fish owls. It has a poorly pronounced pale buff facial disc with white eyebrows, a brown-and-buff back and a buff front, streaked with dark brown. It lives in wet habitats in Southeast Asia, particularly liking coastal forest and mangrove. Its staple diet is fish, but it will eat the carrion of animals up to the size of crocodiles. This owl has unfeathered legs and the soles of its feet have spiny scales, evolutionary developments that help it to catch and keep hold of slimy aquatic creatures. It normally swoops on fish from perches, but can waddle around in the shallows searching for prey with its feet. Birds that set up territory near fish ponds are sometimes killed by man, as they are perceived as a threat to the owner's livelihood. Nest sites include old raptor nests or perhaps a spot hidden amongst the fronds of a bird's nest fern.

PEL'S FISH OWL *Scotopelia peli*
length 24 in (61 cm) wingspan 58 in (147 cm)

This is the largest of the fish owls and differs from most of them in that it has no ear tufts and no facial disc. Two ebony-colored eyes punctuate its soft, round orange head. Its plumage is orangey-brown, paler on the front, with thin black chevron markings all over. The plumage color and barring does vary between individuals, with some birds having some wholly white or black feathers. The immature bird is paler. One of the male's calls is a deep grunt, which can be heard up to two miles (3.2 km) away. This is useful for keeping in contact, as the species inhabits thick forest near rivers and lakes. It is found in Africa, south of the Sahara Desert. The majority of its diet is fish, but it will gulp down the occasional frog, crab, mussel, or insect. The owl catches the fish at the surface of the water, gliding down once it has detected their ripples. Some fish, called "squeakers," may be detected from the sound they make when they grate their fin bones together. The raptor can also wade about in the shallows in search of prey. Its young hatch when fish are at their greatest concentrations, toward the end of the dry season. Although not globally threatened, it is rare in parts of its range. In severe droughts it might not attempt to breed and any young birds that are raised may have trouble finding a suitable patch of river to fish. One of the main threats to this species is the felling of forest.

GREAT-HORNED OWL *Bubo virginianus*

length 22 in (56 cm) wingspan 48 in (122 cm)

One of the most widespread owls in North America, the Great-Horned Owl has long ear tufts and a rusty facial disc. Its plumage can range from pale to dark gray in color. Its hooting call sounds similar to "You awake? Me too." This raptor can survive in a more diverse range of habitats than any other owl species, its success being attributable to several factors: it has no competitors, it can eat a wide variety of different-sized prey, it will nest anywhere suitable, and is reasonably tolerant of humans. It can attack prey

larger than itself and has been known to attempt to catch pet cats. It will even attack humans if they get too close to the nest. The breeding season is between December and July and females have been seen incubating eggs in freezing conditions. This owl can live for many years; one known wild bird survived to the ripe old age of 28.

● WOOD OWLS
24 species

TAWNY OWL *Strix aluco*
length 16 in (41 cm) wingspan 39 in (99 cm)

This medium-sized, compact owl has broad wings and a large, rounded head. Its color is variable, with both gray and brown phases. The facial disc is plain and it has two white "extra eyebrows." One of the most common owls in Europe, North Africa, and the Middle East, its "toowit toowoo" and shrill shriek calls are familiar to many. It lives in wooded areas, including parkland and cemeteries. It hunts for rodents and insects from perches, dropping noiselessly onto the unsuspecting victim. Pairs bond for life and bigamy is very rare. It nests in the holes of old trees and becomes very defensive of the nest site, attacking any intruders, including humans. The Tawny Owl is infamous for taking out one of the eyes of the late Eric Hoskings, one of the pioneers of bird photography, while he was trying to photograph the species at a nest site. Older, larger chicks will eat younger chicks if the food supply becomes short.

URAL OWL *Strix uralensis*

length 24 in (61 cm)
wingspan 51 in (130 cm)

A largish, pale gray-brown owl with darker streaks and bars and pale facial disc, this species inhabits the forest and woodland from eastern Europe and Siberia to Japan. It hunts mainly from perches, looking and listening for small mammals and birds, and can even detect the sound made by voles under 12 inches (30 cm) of snow. Pairs normally form bonds for life, and research has shown that there is only a three per cent "divorce" rate. The period of time between the eggs being laid and the young being independent of their parents is around five months. Any surplus food caught is often stored by or near the nest, but if food is scarce the female may stop incubating her eggs altogether. The Ural Owl is renowned for its fearlessness and will readily attack any intruders, including humans that have come too close to the nest or the young. It aims for the eyes. The population of this species is not globally threatened. Although the population does fluctuate, numbers increase after good vole years.

SPOTTED OWL *Strix occidentalis*

length 17 in (43 cm)
wingspan 47 in (119 cm)

This is a medium-sized brown owl with many white spots. It lives in dense, wet, mature forests and wooded canyons in western North America and northern Mexico. Its diet is varied and includes small to medium-sized mammals, birds, reptiles, amphibians, and insects. It will even hunt for smaller owls and is able catch bats and insects in midair,  although most hunting is from suitable perches. After detecting the victim with its excellent hearing or eyesight, the owl swoops over to grab the prey. It nests in trees or cliff ledges and can use an old squirrel or crow nest. The female lays up to four eggs and it takes about two months before the young are ready to leave the nest. This is a long-lived bird, with some ringed birds reaching 17 years old. It is uncommon or endangered over much of its range, due to the restricted nature of its specialized habitat, which is under continual threat from tree felling. The increasing population of Barred Owls is also thought to be having a negative effect on the Spotted Owl through competition for prey and potential hybridization.

133

BARRED OWL *Strix varia*

length 21 in (53 cm) wingspan 55 in (140 cm)

This large brown owl is quite similar to the closely related Spotted Owl. It is a lighter brown with a paler front, which has brown barring and is streaked below the chest. The facial disc is whiter. Its song sounds like "Who cooks for you, who cooks for you all?" It is a common owl, found in mature forest and woods, often next to open countryside. Its range extends across North America to Mexico. Often active during daytime, it eats a wide variety of prey: small mammals, birds, reptiles, amphibians, fish, crabs, and insects. One race even eats baby armadillos and alligators. Although it normally hunts from a perch from which it pounces on its prey, it can hover and can wade around in the shallows, striking out with its talons to grasp prey, which is then pulled to shore. This species has expanded westward, and may be causing problems for the rarer Spotted Owl.

CHACO OWL *Strix chacoensis*

length 15 in (38 cm)
wingspan 38 in (97 cm)

The Chaco Owl is found in the Chaco region of Bolivia, Paraguay, and Argentina in South America. Chaco is the name given to the dense dry scrub and woodland, often populated with cacti, in this area. The adult has dark gray-brown barring to the front, a dark brown back with thin white bars, and dark wings with cream and white spots. The youngster is paler with more diffuse bars. It hunts for small birds, mammals, and reptiles from suitable perches, and will also eat scorpions, large spiders, and centipedes. This species nests in a tree cavity and the female lays up to three eggs. It takes about two and a half months from the time the eggs are laid until the young leave the nest. There is no information about this raptor's population size, but, although not globally threatened, it is thought to be uncommon over most of its range. The biology of this owl is not well known.

GRAY OWL *Strix nebulosa*

length 29 in (74 cm) wingspan 55 in (140 cm)

This is one of the largest owls and it is the biggest in size found in North America, although the Great Horned Owl is heavier. It has a huge head and neck and can appear top-heavy in flight. It has large facial discs with gray concentric rings surrounding the small-looking yellow eyes. Its huge wingspan is enhanced by slow, majestic wing beats. It lives in the boreal forests of North America, northern Europe, and Siberia. Often hunting in the day, it will pounce on small mammals. It can locate them by listening to the sounds they make, even if they are below 18 inches (45 cm) of snow or an inch (2 cm) of soil, using its exceptional hearing. The population of this owl fluctuates in a close

relationship with the numbers of its prey. In a good vole year there will be improved breeding success. It usually nests on tree stumps, in a disused raptor nest, or even on the ground. This owl becomes very aggressive toward any intruders venturing near the nest site and will attack animals as large as black bears. The female can lay up to nine eggs in a good vole year but normally lays between three and six. This species can be cannibalistic; the older brothers or sisters sometimes eat the youngest chick, particularly if insufficient food is brought to the nest.

137

SPECTACLED OWL *Pulsatrix perspicillata*
length 19 in (48 cm) wingspan 44 in (112 cm)

This striking large owl is found in tropical forest and wooded habitats in South and Central America. It has a dark back and buff-white front, dark head, and dark facial disc with contrasting white brows, whiskers, and chin. The juvenile looks different from its parents, with an all-white body. It can take up to five years for an immature bird to get all its adult feathers. The Spectacled Owl eats a wide variety of vertebrate prey up to the size of opossums and skunks, and will also go for crabs and for insects such as beetles and caterpillars. It hunts the prey by spotting it from a suitable perch. The female lays two to three eggs in a tree cavity, but usually only one young survives to fledging and is cared for by the parents for up to a year.

● **PYGMY OWLS AND OWLETS**
38 species

CENTRAL AMERICAN PYGMY OWL
Glaucidium griseiceps
length 6 in (15 cm) wingspan 14 in (36 cm)

As its name suggests, this is a very small owl found in Central America. It has a dark rufous back and a white-and-rufous front. The round head, which has no ear tufts, is pale brown-gray with fine white spots.

In common with other pygmy owls, it has two dark patches on the nape of its neck. These look like eyes and may confuse predators into thinking that the owl is always looking at them. It is found in humid rainforests and semi-open countryside, where it hunts for small mammals and birds, as well as the odd reptile and large insect. It nests in tree cavities and will use old woodpecker nests. Although classified as "not globally threatened" there is little data on its actual population size. This raptor used to be known as a Least Pygmy Owl but this species was recently split into three: the Central American Pygmy Owl, the Tamaulipa Pygmy-Owl, and the Colima Pygmy Owl.

ELF OWL *Micrathene whitneyi*
length 6 in (13 cm) wingspan 15 in (38 cm)

This, the smallest owl in the world, is only about the size of a chubby sparrow. It is dark brown above with a couple of rows of white spots. The cinnamon-brown round head has no ear tufts. The front is also cinnamon-brown, becoming whiter toward the belly. It has a surprisingly loud, yelping, puppylike song, which may be repeated for long periods. The Elf Owl can live in a variety of woodland habitats, including cactus desert, and eats insects such as moths, crickets, and beetles, as well as spiders and scorpions. It can nab flying insects by using its feet and can even hover when necessary. It does not need to drink, obtaining all the fluid it needs from its diet. It often roosts and nests in woodpecker holes in cacti. It can take as little as seven weeks from the time the eggs are laid for the young to leave the nest. The youngsters can catch insects as soon as they can fly.

LITTLE OWL *Athene noctua*
length 8 in (20 cm) wingspan 22 in (56 cm)

The Little Owl is a small, spotted, pale brown-and-white owl found across Europe, Asia and North Africa. It ekes out a living from open countryside in such diverse habitats as stony desert or lush farmland. It probably did not colonize western Europe until the forest was cleared in the Middle Ages; it was introduced in the UK toward the end of the nineteenth century. It can eat a wide variety of prey, ranging from earthworms to small mammals. The Little Owl will usually drop on to its victim from a perch, but can hover and run after things on the ground. It often roosts in the day in the open, especially during the breeding season, when it may be on the lookout for potential intruders. Although it nests in holes in trees, it can utilize holes in buildings, or even rabbit burrows. The population of the Little Owl fluctuates, decreasing after severe winters. In Europe, recent declines are due to intensified farming, leading to the loss of suitable breeding sites.

NORTHERN HAWK OWL *Strix ulula*

length 15 in (38 cm) wingspan 33 in (84 cm)

This distinctive hawklike owl often perches on top of tree stumps and conifers, slowly raising and lowering its long tail. Its back is dark brown with pale markings, while the front is pale with fine bars. It has a white face outlined in black, and penetrating yellow eyes. It usually hunts during the day, eating birds up to the size of grouse, and mammals as large as a hare, but prefers to eat small voles. It is uncommon over most of its range in the northern latitudes of Siberia, North America, and Europe and its populations fluctuate with availability of prey. It is often very tame, but will attack humans and other perceived threats if they get too close to the nest or to young birds that have just left the nest by raking the intruder with its talons. It may sometimes adopt a distraction display to entice any potential predator away from the nest by flopping onto the ground with its wings spread out as if it was injured. It then flutters along the ground, calling. It can lay up to 13 eggs in good vole years.

BURROWING OWL *Athene cunicularia*
length 10 in (25 cm) wingspan 22 in (56 cm)

This long-legged, short-tailed, ground-loving owl uses the deserted burrows of prairie dogs and ground squirrels for breeding and roosting. It lives in open grassland across South and North America, including golf courses and airports. It is brown with white and pale spots above and pale with brown barring below. The brown-and-white spotted head has no ear tufts. The race found in central and eastern Brazil has an orangey wash to the plumage. It eats mostly small mammals and insects, the latter being caught during the hours of daylight, often in midair. This

144

raptor can also catch prey on foot and can hover in flight when necessary. It nests in a burrow, which is often lined with dung. Although some build their own burrows from scratch, chipping away with their bills and kicking earth back with their feet, most take the easy option and renovate an old burrow. The female can lay up to ten eggs, which hatch in three to four weeks. If provoked, the young have a call that sounds like the hiss of a rattlesnake, which is often enough to deter most predators. The population in some areas is declining due to road casualties and, perhaps more significantly, to the eradication of prairie dogs and ground squirrels, whose burrows are so essential for the species' survival.

FOREST OWLET *Athene blewitti*
length 9 in (23 cm) wingspan 21 in (53 cm)

The Forest Owlet is a critically endangered species found only in India. It was rediscovered as recently as 1997 in northwest Maharashta and had been thought to be extinct since the last one was collected in 1884. It is a smallish, distinctive owl with a white-and-black barred belly, and a sun-bleached chocolate-brown back and wings, which are speckled with white. The head and breast are gray-brown. Its flight is direct, with no undulation. It is found in lowland forest, a habitat that is often under threat of destruction. Little is known of the bird's biology, so there is no information available about its breeding habits. The few observations that have been made have established that it hunts during the hours of daylight and often perches prominently in the top of trees, regularly flicking its tail. There is little information about this species' diet but it is known to include lizard.

● HAWK OWLS
21 species

BARKING OWL OR WINKING OWL

Ninox connivens
length 16 in (41 cm) wingspan 40 in (102 cm)
This medium-sized hawk owl is found in Australia and New Guinea. It has an indistinct facial disc and its plumage is brown with white spots above and pale brown or orangey streaks below. As well as a gruff woof, similar to a dog's bark, it can emit a cry that sounds like a long, strangled scream. It lives in forest, woodland, and savannah with open areas. It hunts prey from the size of large insects to mammals as big as an opossum and can catch bats and insects by grabbing them with its talons in midair. It normally nests in a hollow in a tree but will occasionally nest on a branch, in a fork of a tree, or even on the ground. Pairs or family groups often roost together. It has declined in southeastern Australia due to habitat loss caused by tree clearance and overgrazing.

● **EARED OWLS**
9 species

LONG-EARED OWL

Asio otus
length 14 in (36 cm)
wingspan 37 in (94 cm)

This eye-catching owl is found in the countries that wrap around the globe from North America across Europe to Siberia. In winter, many fly southward to avoid freezing Arctic conditions in the northern part of their range. Easily overlooked, this owl roosts during the day in dense cover, often in small groups, sometimes with as many as 20 other birds. Its plumage is a luxuriant mixture of golden-buff and rufous-brown tones, which are perfect for camouflage when hiding in trees. It has striking, fierce orange eyes and two tufts of feathers, referred to as "ears," on the top of its head. Its real ears are on the side of its head, covered by other feathers. This species is less likely to hunt during the day than some other owls, such as the Barn Owl, but will do so if it has to feed its young. It can detect its favored food, small rodents such as voles, in total darkness. It has been known for two Long-Eared Owls to work together when hunting roosting birds. One owl frightens a sleeping bird on one side of a hedge, while the other waits on the other side for the startled bird to emerge. This owl has even been known to drag its talons through water in an attempt to catch fish. If disturbed at its nest site, an adult will sometimes drop to the ground, wings flapping, and then drag itself off with one wing, so as to distract the intruder from its eggs and young.

SHORT-EARED OWL *Asio flammeus*
length 15 in (38 cm) wingspan 40 in (102 cm)

A medium-sized owl with small ear tufts, the Short-Eared Owl's plumage is mottled brown and buff above and paler underneath. It often hunts in the day and is identifiable by its distinctive buoyant, flapping flight. It has a huge range over open countryside in the Americas, Europe, Asia, and Africa. Prone to wander, it has even colonized many remote Pacific islands. It hunts for small mammals, such as voles, by flying slowly over suitable habitat, hovering where necessary, and can detect its quarry using its excellent hearing. It nests on the ground, unusual for an owl, and constructs a nest by trampling vegetation to form a platform, which is then lined with grass and downy feathers. The female can vary the number of eggs laid. In years when there are good numbers of voles it may lay up to ten eggs, whereas in average years only four or five are laid.

STRIPED OWL *Asio clamator*

length 15 in (38 cm) wingspan 40 in (102 cm)

The Striped Owl is a brown, upright owl, with long ear tufts and a black-bordered, whitish facial disc. It is a camouflaged brown, black, and buff above and paler below with dark brown streaks. It can survive in an unusually wide variety of habitats across South and Central America, ranging from tropical rainforest to plantations and suburban gardens. It hunts either by quartering open countryside in flight or by dropping on to prey from perches, and can eat a large assortment of species, from insects to birds and rodents. The Striped Owl nests on the ground or in a tree and the female lays up to three eggs, which take about a month to hatch. Although it is not globally threatened, its actual status is poorly known, but it is thought to be a local and uncommon species. There is little information on its biology or ecology, which is surprising as it is often found in suburban areas and farms.

▶ **SAW-WHET OWLS**

4 species

TENGMALM'S OWL OR BOREAL OWL

Aegolius funereus

length 10 in (25 cm) wingspan 23 in (58 cm)

The Tengmalm's Owl is a smallish species with distinct white facial discs outlined in black. It hunts in the forests of North America, Europe, and Siberia, on the lookout for insects, birds, and small mammals. It first spots its quarry from a perch and will then wait several minutes until its victim moves into a vulnerable situation before pouncing. It can detect prey under snow and vegetation using its superb hearing. It nests in tree cavities or old woodpecker holes. The female can lay as many as 11 eggs and can raise more than one brood per season in good vole years. Pairs are usually monogamous for each breeding season, but it is probably not uncommon for the male or female to have other partners. Females and immature birds migrate away from the breeding sites and will erupt southward if there is a crash in the rodent population. This tends to happen every four years. The population of this species can decline after the removal of mature old trees with suitable nest holes, although this can be overcome by providing nest boxes. Up to 11,000 boxes have been erected in Finland and are thought to house 90 percent of the population there.

● **NORTHERN SAW-WHET OWL** *Aegolius acadicus*
length 7 in (18 cm) wingspan 18 in (46 cm)
This small owl is found in the woodlands of North and
Central America and is at its most common in coniferous
forest. It has pretty orangey blotches on its front and a
brown back with some white spots. The head is a paler
brown with short white streaks. Its name comes from the
sound of one of its calls, which is remarkably similar to that
produced by filing, or "whetting," a large saw. This repetitive
song can be heard up to half a mile (0.8 km) away. It eats
small mammals, such as deer mice, and will take small
birds, particularly during migration, when they are active at
night. It will often nest in woodpecker holes and will use
nest boxes. The population of this owl is probably slowly
declining due to loss of habitat from forest clearance. New
coniferous forest is often too thick and lacks the clearings
and open understory necessary for good hunting.

GLOSSARY

Accipiter. The scientific name of a genus of the family Accipitridae.

Aerie. The lofty nest or nest site of a bird of prey. Sometimes spelled "eyrie".

Air sac. An air-filled space in a bird that forms a connection between the lungs and bone cavities, and aids in breathing and temperature regulation.

Alula. A small joint in the middle of a bird's wing, similar to human thumb and bearing three or four quill-like feathers. Also known as the bastard wing or spurious wing.

Arboreal. A bird that lives in trees.

Auriculars. Feathers around the ear. Also called ear coverts.

Aves. Scientific class of vertebrata for birds, derived from the Latin word for bird, *avis*.

Axillaries. Feathers along the underside of the wings, where they connect to the body. Concealed by the closed wing.

Barring. Narrow bands of contrasting color.

Boreal. Being of the north; of northern areas or distribution.

Buteo. Common name for a group of large, soaring hawks with broad wings in the genus Buteo.

Carrion. The dead and rotting body of an animal.

Cere. A soft, fleshy area at the base of the upper bill, which contains the nostrils.

Classification. Arranging or grouping of animals and plants into smaller and smaller groups in the this sequence: class, order, family, genus, species.

Clutch. Set of eggs laid by one bird in one breeding attempt.

Crepuscular. Birds that are active during dawn and dusk.

Crest. Long feathers found on the top of a bird's head.

DDT. [Dichlorodiphenyltrichioroethane] An insecticide that is also toxic to animals and humans. Damaging to the envirnoment; tends to affect the repoductive process in animals. It has been banned in the United States since 1972.

Diurnal. Animals that usually feed and are more active during the daytime. Opposite of nocturnal.

Eye-ring. A circle around the eye.

Falconiformes. One of the two orders of the Aves class that are birds of prey (the other being Strigiformes). Falconiformes are divided into a further four groups, called families. These are the Cathartidae, the Accipitres, the Sagittariidae, and the Falcones. The Accipitres family has the greatest number of species. Chiefly diurnal.

Fledge. To acquire the feathers needed for flight.

Fledgling. A young bird.

Flight feathers. The large feathers on the wing that are broken down into primaries, (on the far joint of a bird's wing), secondaries, (found between the body and the primaries), and tertials (a group of feathers on the wing, found closest to the birds body).

Gape. Base of the bill where the mandibles join.

Gizzard. The stomach of a bird, which has thick muscular walls. As birds cannot chew, they may swallow grit to grind up food particles and therefore aid food digestion.

Gleaning. Foraging for food.

Hawking. To make an attack while on the wing, usually taking insects.

Hybridization. The mixing of different animals or plants of different species.

Immature bird. Young bird in its first plumage after molting its juvenile feathers; has not yet developed adult feathers. The immature plumage can be very similar to that of the adult.

Juvenile. A young bird in its first covering of feathers, after molting its initial down.

Keratin. A tough fibrous material. In birds, it is present in feathers and the tough outer coatings of the bill, leg scales, and claws.

Kleptoparisitism. The act of stealing prey from other species.

Lore. The sides of the face between the bottom of the eye and the base of the bill.

Malar stripes. The area in front of, and slightly below, the eye. Most species of falcons have dark malar stripes down from the front part of the eyes, which may reduce sun glare.

Migration. Movement from one area to another, usually with the seasons. This allows for the exploitation of new food sources or change of habitat.

Molt. Replacement of old feathers with new ones.

Montane. Pertaining to mountainous terrain.

Nape. The back of a bird's head. Also called the hindneck.

Nestling period. The time between the young bird hatching and taking its first flight.

Nictitating membrane. A clear, vertical fold that effectively forms a third eyelid. Can protect the eye without affecting vision.

Nomadic. Tends to travel or roam frequently.

Pathogen. Any disease-producing agent.

Plumage. The light waterproof coating on a bird, that consists of the feathers covering the head, neck, and body, the tail feathers, the wing feathers and the down that lies beneath. Breeding plumage is a feather molt from winter plumage. It typically consists of brighter colors, sometimes with ornaments or frills – usually to attract opposite sex. Winter plumage is a seasonal molt; normally duller colors.

Polyandry. A practice where a female mates with more than one male, sometimes as many as five. An example may include the Harris Hawk. If a single male mates with more than one female the situation is called polygyny.

Rufous. Of a yellowish red or brownish red color.

Quartering. Methodically covering an area of ground for prey.

Stoop. The spectacular, rapid dive of the hunting bird of prey.

Strigiformes. Owls. Divided into two families: Tytonidae (barn owls) and Strigidae (typical owls).

Supercilium. The arch, or line of feathers above each eye.

Tarsus. The part of the leg that is just above the foot.

Territory. Area where a bird normally lives and feeds, and can be defended fiercely.

Thermals. A rising current of warm air, which soaring birds use to gain height.

Trousers. A characteristic where the bird has thick, short legs, which are feathered towards the top.

Vertebrates. Animals with a backbone.

INDEX

INDEX